Imitating C........ ....
guided Changework

To Mum & Dad
love

Imitating Christ through guided Changework

Ian Field

Highland Books

Godalming, Surrey

First published in 2001 by Highland Books, Two High Pines, Knoll Road, Godalming, Surrey GU7 2EP.

ISBN: 1-897913-60-5

Printed in the UK by Omnia Books Limited, Bishopbriggs, Glasgow.

*For Bev, you not only speak the truth in love,
you embody it*

*Hannah, Ben & Tom, just when I thought life couldn't
get any better – I got you!*

*With thanks to my brother,
my friends at Harborough Evangelical Church,
and Connie Wilkins
for all the support.*

Contents

FOREWORD

Jesus pioneered a "new way". The disciples followed in his footsteps, for after the resurrection appearances of Jesus, they went forth and turned the world upside down with the message "He is alive". The Apostle Paul pioneered the taking of the Gospel to the Gentile world risking and receiving vast persecution from his countrymen.

Once in a while the Church today produces a pioneer – someone willing to "step out" and take a chance by proclaiming to the world new ideas and new concepts to enhance the lives of the Followers of Christ. Martin Luther pioneered when he nailed his thesis on the door of the church. Others of the Protestant Reformation pioneered new ideas and new concepts in proclaiming the Gospel of Christ. The many leaders of the modern Pastoral Care movement pioneered in introducing Christians to the scientific discoveries of human psychic. Following that level of thinking, Rev. Ian Field has dared to pioneer in his new book Imitating Christ Through Guided Changework.

In this work, Ian pulls the "meat" out of the relatively new cognitive model called Neuro-Linguistic (NLP) and wraps these powerful tools up with the Word of God and challenges the reader to model the life of Christ in his or her thinking and behaviour. Not buying into the oft held belief that thought patterns are solidified in concrete and therefore unchangeable, Ian demonstrates that thought patterns contrary to the will of God are not only changeable but the author provides the tools to change them.

Careful always to uphold the "Truth" of the Word of God, Ian expertly walks the reader through the many patterns and structure of this revolutionary model and maps out a plan for the reader to follow in "renewing his or her mind" into the mind of Christ. Such renewing allows the reader to take those old "bitter roots" (Hebrews 12:15) and to bring to bear the

Truths of Christ on to those bitter roots thus rendering them powerless. Such exercises enable one to "put on the mind of Christ" and to behave in ways that honor our Lord.

Ian is to be congratulated for packaging this revolutionary material in such a readable and Biblically understandable fashion.

Bobby G. Bodenhamer, D.Min.
Gastonia, North Carolina, December 2000

Part One

The Reasons 'Why'

The Theory behind the Practice

Chapter 1

Imitation of Christ – the invitation to imitation

Have you ever wondered if penguins dream in black and white? Does what they see in others around them set boundaries for their hopes, dreams and desires? Maybe not – but in years of church pastoral ministry, also in working as a counsellor for the National Health Service, and as a prison chaplain I know that people can be like penguins! Whether I am addressing groups at Spring Harvest or in my local secondary school I always have individuals come up to me afterwards with the same heart-breaking tale: the details may differ, but they have ended up a penguin. People who have been made in the very image and likeness of God find themselves scratching around living lives of quiet desperation with monochrome dreams learnt from the next man (or the ad-man!).

All of us get 'stuck', no matter how mature we may be, whether we are leaders, counsellors or people-helpers. We hear the command of scripture to 'put off' ungodliness, and 'put on' new thinking, feeling and behaving (Col 3.1-10), but feel unable to. As we look around our Churches, families and workplaces, we discover a national epidemic of 'stuckness'. The pressures and demands of modern-day life will not allow most of us to pursue godliness in peaceful monastic surroundings, so we need to learn new ways to 'unstick' ourselves and the others we care for, to restore movement and growth in our lives. The new tools you are about to learn are not 'instead of' the ways you have already learned that work, but 'as well as' – if you, or anyone you know has ever been stuck, then you know that what you really need are more choices, by the end of this book you will have new mental, emotional and communication flexibility to help yourself and those you care for to have more choice in life.

Many of us start with unlimited dreams, as children we know we have a place and a purpose, we are here to play our part, we can be what we want and we may even change the world! Through the years, however, we experience the pains of frustration and disappointment, or sometimes even the pain of 'success', and in our desire to avoid future pain, we lower our standards, sell out on our dreams and bury our destiny alive. This book is a wake-up call, a set of tools and approaches to help you dust off your dream, to regain your vision – it's time to live the High Life! Its time to raise your sights, to regain hope and a sense of your destiny. The High Life is not just for you, but all those you know and care about – here are skills to help you transform your life, and those around you.

Jesus had a dream, a vision and a purpose, He wants us to imitate Him – using the cutting-edge tools in this book you can make a quantum leap in Christlikeness, life and power – it is not humble to stumble around in failure, God's will for you is to be blessed and be a blessing. Jesus is not worried that you will become so much like Him that He will lose His job! He wants you to throw yourself unreservedly into the High Life, and the way to start that is by following Him …

Not Ought, but MUST!

Imitating or modelling Christ is not an optional extra, it isn't even something we *should* do, it is a *must*. If we are not actively involved in the process of becoming more Christlike we need to stop and ask ourselves what we think we are doing! Jesus became very frustrated with his followers when they began to see discipleship in terms of status, ritual or self interest (Mark 10.14-15,35-45). Settle it for yourself now: does Jesus call you to follow him, yes or no? Does he expect you to learn from him and obey him, yes or no? Finally, does the whole New Testament insist that you become like him, in your words, actions, thoughts, attitudes and being, yes or no? The answer to all three questions is the same, Christlikeness is a must.

While the call of Jesus is enough to motivate us in the pursuit of Christlikeness, also consider these questions:

- why is it that Father God wants you to become like Jesus?
- what will he be able to give to you through this process?
- what does he know about Christlikeness that makes him able to equate it with the joys of heaven?
- how do you feel in your relationship with God as you become like Jesus?
- why is it good for you to become like Jesus?
- who will you really be when you *really* become like Jesus?
- why is it good for others if you become like Jesus?
- what positive impact do you make on your family and community by becoming like Jesus?

By now you can *feel totally convinced* that not only is Christlikeness a must, but also very desirable, it is the path to our greatest fulfilment because it is what we were created for – to reflect the image of God again (Gen 1.28, Eph 4.23-24). The next step is to see who is responsible for this change, is it us or God? The best way to answer this is to turn to the Bible and look at Jesus and the first disciples: the initiative lay with Jesus calling the disciples, so also in our lives, the initiative is always God's, we could never have been saved had he not called us and drawn us to himself. But the gospels do not stop there, the disciples were no passive recipients of God's grace and calling, they had actively to respond – so do we. I like to think of our discipleship walk more like a dance: God moves and we respond, he definitely has the lead. If it were not for God then nothing could happen at all ('apart from me you can do nothing' Jn 15.5) but if we do not respond then we are capable of 'quenching the Spirit's work in our lives' (1 Thess 5.19). The disciples had the responsibility to pay attention, to learn and assimilate, to ask questions when necessary and to go when sent – the very fact that Jesus sometimes got frustrated when they didn't 'get it' is proof that discipleship wasn't done *to* them by him.

But if we are going to take some responsibility for change, don't we run the risk of self effort – of relying on our own works and strength for righteousness? Doesn't the Bible say 'that which is flesh is flesh'? and that the flesh can produce no good thing (Rom 7 & 8). Doesn't Paul say that it is 'God at work within you, to do his will'? This is a vital question for us to answer, because we will not give ourselves totally to having God's will fully realised in us until we know who gets the glory for the changes that take place in our lives – surely if we are involved we will begin to boast. What about 'let go and let God' are we to be passive recipients of God's grace for fear of adding 'flesh' to it? We can be certain that anything of value is initiated and sustained by God and that in our own strength we can no more become Christlike than we could save ourselves. However, the Bible also exhorts us to 'offer up our bodies as living sacrifices' (Rom 12.1-2) we are to do the offering, we are to 'gird up the loins of our minds' (1 Pet 1.13) and to 'put off the old man and put on Christ' (Eph 4.22-24). To be totally passive and expect God to 'do it to us' is not Biblical and will yield little or no growth. To be totally proactive, driving what we think God should do in our lives, or even that we can do it ourselves is presumption. The way ahead for us is to respond to God's loving initiative, learn from him what he is wanting to do, and then in humble faith co-operate with him. Many words have been written about the dynamic relationship between faith, grace and works: my intention is to highlight the issue for you to wrestle with, so 'over to you'.

Have you been passive, giving up your God-given responsibility and power away? Honestly, have you looked to others for your spiritual growth? People in your church, your leaders, friends or those who teach truth to you? Have you sat like a 'pew potato' watching others serve and exercise their gifts and wonder why they got the growth and you didn't? Or how about the opposite extreme: have you been rushing around trying to do all sorts of things for God, do you set high standards (even perfection) and then strive like crazy to achieve them, only to feel exhausted, disappointed and guilty when you fail? Do you start projects in God's name, only to feel a terrific burden that God doesn't seem to alleviate; or how about looking at other Christians and comparing yourself with them to see if you are better than them or not?

These traps both come from the mistake of making responsibility exclusive to either God or man – whereas true discipleship is an ongoing relationship of following Jesus and 'dancing' responsively into Christlikeness. If you have been taking too much responsibility, it is time to trust; if you have been too passive, it is time to obey.

> 'Trust and obey, for there's no other way,
> to be happy in Jesus, than to trust and obey'

If you can now say to yourself that Christlikeness is <u>a must</u>, that *you* must do it (out of your relationship to Jesus), the last step is to know that becoming like Jesus is a divine possibility, it is not 'pie in the sky' but the most compelling vision a human can have. It makes real and personal the question 'what would Jesus do?' as we not only find that we can envisage the answer in our own lives but increasingly find that we are automatically doing those things because we are becoming Christlike in our thinking, feeling and believing.

Jesus is more than a historical character

So how is it possible to become like Jesus? How can we learn to think and feel and act like him? If God has taken the initiative to call us to Christlikeness, what is our response? We come back to the invitation to imitation, or, in modern terms – modelling. Modelling is only a deliberate way of learning, it is what any apprentice would do. It is crucial to remember that when we are modelling Jesus we are not just imitating a historical figure, Jesus is alive and present with you. We have more than just a book of instructions, the Holy Spirit makes Jesus' presence available to you. As we allow the Holy Spirit to lead us we can keep in mind that he is the same Spirit who shaped and trained Jesus as a man (Lk 2.52,4.1,14) and is wanting to do the same in us if we will let him.

In order to model anyone we have to be with them. Jesus is able to be present and reveal facets of himself through the Bible (the gospels in particular), through our neighbour (Matt 25.37-40), in communion (Lk 22.19-20) and in our hearts (Jn 14.23). The first place for us to know the thinking, feeling and doing of Jesus is the Bible, and we are able to begin modelling him in the loving atmosphere he creates (Matt 11.29) 'learn from me for I am humble and gentle in heart, and you shall find rest for your souls', he stimulates faith that he is more than a perfect man who is to be our example – he is our brother, redeemer and friend, who has total love and commitment to us, he is with us always and everywhere.

Christlikeness needs to become an obsession for us, modelling on Jesus means taking him as our ultimate goal in life, moulding our lives into his pattern, not the world's (Rom 12.2) and bringing our lives into conformity to his. There is joy unspeakable, power, passion and fulfilment most people only dream of – this is Gods will for you. Imagine how your life will change, being like Jesus isn't just good for you, it is also the best expression of love – if you are behaving like Jesus your life will be a constant blessing to your brothers and sisters and those who touch your life.

The place where we all start is in hearing the call of Christ to follow him (Matt 4.18-22) and responding to it in faith and obedience. From there we discover what he has in mind. Jesus offered himself as a model – more than a teacher with only knowledge to impart, he wants us to learn from him how to think, feel and behave. Jesus had almost certainly worked as a carpenter with his father Joseph, and so we can assume he had been a *'mathētēs'*, apprentice of his father. How would he learn? by being with his father, paying attention, learning how to approach tasks and also the specific skills and behaviours that produce good carpentry. In short, a disciple learns by modelling the teacher who has already got the skills they desire – they do not have to reinvent the wheel or go through years of trial and error. This is the call of Jesus, but not to learn carpentry, rather to be like him.

Jesus repeatedly emphasised that he wanted his disciples to go beyond replicating his actions to the forming of the attitudes and identity that he operated from. After washing his disciples' feet he said, 'I have given you an example, so that what I have done, you also may do' (Jn 13.15). He then teaches about love and a servant's heart. In the invitation to imitation we discover there is a family likeness to be developed, as children of God we will look like our 'older brother' (Eph 5.1). Peter encourages us to 'walk in his steps' (1 Pet 2.21) again emphasising attitudes as well as behaviour. Paul speaks teleologically when he writes that our destiny is to be conformed to the image of Jesus (Rom

8.29), and we are exhorted to model on those who have imitated Christ (1 Cor. 11.1; 1 Thess. 1.6; Phil. 3.17; 4.9)

If it's not from your core it will fizzle.

Discipleship is able to impact differing levels of our person – we can focus on the level of environment and campaign as 'green' Christians, and surely God has given us the mandate to tend and keep His world (Gen 1.28-31). We could look at the level of behaviours, ranging from the individual spiritual disciplines of prayer, fasting and meditation, through to ministry to the poor and oppressed, asking the question 'what are we going to do about it?' In response to this question there have been some outstanding works done, individually and organisationally. The importance of action needs constantly re-emphasising, and yet some of the projects fizzled out or the people involved would just drop out because if we undertake even the most dynamic and Biblical activities, if they are not consistent with our identity, who we are at our 'core', then eventually we will revert to how we perceive ourselves. Those ministries and works which have flourished and have been sustained through time have done so because they are congruent with the person or organisation's 'self image', and are an expression of that identity, rather than just an activity. As an example, if you were to take a rubber band and hold it loosely over your thumb and forefinger, it retains its shape and is comfortable; however if you now stretch it apart so that it is pulled out of its natural shape, this could be like undertaking an activity because you know it is 'right', but if you try and keep it like that for the whole day, you will get tired, and if you are distracted at any point and forget, the rubber band will pull your fingers back together and regain its original shape. This simple metaphor explains why sometimes we are unable to keep a habit, work or project going if it does not reflect our 'shape', it is tiring, and tends to 'snap back' when total will-power and attention are not given. The good news is that through God's power we are not what we were and are able to change so that what we do is less fatiguing and more long term.

Another aspect of discipleship is 'authenticity' which seeks to integrate and incorporate Christian beliefs and values into all areas of life – the importance of a holistic discipleship, rather than will power and action. We can explore ways of godly marriage, parenting, health, diet and career, there is no human activity which is outside the sphere of Christ's influence. As we do this we learn about Jesus' values and beliefs which equip us more for life and create a greater sense of well- being as well as consistency in our actions.

There is a saying, 'Operari sequitur esse' which means 'our actions stem from our being'. Some people will try to form their identity by what they do, but truth be told, if we try to take actions that are inconsistent with our sense of identity we will find it difficult, tiring and soon stop. But what if we could change our identity so radically, so drastically that new behaviours and attitudes, ones that support us and are consistent with our Christian faith automatically flow from it and continually reinforce that new self image more and more? What is this identity, this destiny that is so exciting? Our destiny, the goal of our discipleship is more than a set of actions, more even than a set of capabilities – it is Christlikeness. When we begin to understand the implications of this simple word, we are set on fire, knowing that it is the highest, most noble, fulfilling and exciting calling a person could ever have. As we become like Jesus the actions, words, thoughts and miracles flow from who we are, they are not a means to become like Him but are an expression of the reality that we are like Him. The apostle Paul highlights this distinction in 1 Corinthians 13 where he lists the things that can be done, even martyrdom, but if they don't come from inside, from love, from who we really are then they are empty and worthless, whereas the most simple word or action coming from Christlikeness can transform a life and move a mountain.

Master the art of loving:

Fr. L. Gonzales[1] says 'If love is more than a feeling, that is, the firm decision of searching for others excellence, then action is needed in order to facilitate his / her improvement ... loving actions require skills, strategies and techniques – because of that, those who really want to master the art of loving can thrive a lot on NLP (see glossary). This new branch of science empowers the lovers and teaches them how to make the most of their loving decisions'

In the following chapters of this book you will learn new tools to help you master the art of loving, to speed you in your pursuit of holiness and Christlikeness. The tools in this book can be dangerous, like a scalpel they need to be handled carefully, but they can cut through barriers, limitations and ugly 'growths' in your life to allow you to become what Christ desires for you. Leaders, carers and counsellors will find a treasure-trove of techniques to help people change and grow. I believe that the quality of our lives is directly related to the commitment we have to growing and changing as people – we have all we need for that purpose: the secure love of Father God, the strength of the Indwelling Spirit and Jesus as our Saviour and Model, the neurolinguistic tools in these pages will help us take our modelling of Jesus off the pages of the Bible, and into our lives.

Note: The following chapters *use NLP tools to teach NLP*; you will find stories, quotes, puns, loops of recurring thoughts and occasionally non-grammatical or confusing sentence structure – this is intentional, and noticing it is a sign that you are learning correctly.

Chapter 2

Psychology or faith?

Some time ago I was lecturing in a Bible College when I found a book in the library which summarises, I think, many of the concerns of good Christian folk when the discussion turns to psychology, in summary the book said:

- Psychology is a way for man to rely on human ability and strength ('the flesh') for peace of mind, wholeness etc. without any reference to God. Because of this psychology is a system which is at best carnal, at worst anti-God.

- As we look into the history and private lives of some of the people who have developed psychological theories we find that they may have had atheistic or humanistic biases and some of them were downright sinful, therefore psychology is evil.

- If we have a technique which gives a person relief apart from prayer and faith, then prayer, faith and God become redundant, and that unscrupulous therapists may in fact nurture feelings of trust and dependency in themselves by the client.

- Many psychological systems are amoral, with no references to right or wrong, good or bad or any absolute truth and error, in fact psychology is presented as a cult of self pleasing and happiness at all costs which entertains no absolutes at all.

- Finally, some of the claims of 'cures' and successful treatment are dishonest and exaggerated, and are designed to seduce people in pain away from God who alone can help them.

There is some truth in the author's claims, and if they were entirely true I'm sure that all of us would leave the discussion there. What we can say is that there are genuine concerns that we need to deal with, although I personally would not come to the same conclusions that this well-meaning man did. Over the last few decades there have been some respected Christians who have tried to explore and develop Biblical approaches and uses of psychology. Men like Dr James Dobson, Larry Crabb, Frank Minirith, Paul Meier, Roger Hurding and Josh McDowell have done a thorough job of bringing those Christian concerns to bear on the areas of psychology and counselling to see if there is any common ground at all. Some of the characteristics of Biblical counselling which they list are as follows, notice how many of our concerns are fully dealt with:

- God is love (1 Jn 4.16) and God is truth (Jn 14.6), God's truth and love will set us free (Jn 8.31-32) – this enables us to meet people at their point of need, just as Jesus did, and handle issues of false beliefs, rejections, self esteem and behaviours.

- Though not all crises or problems are spiritual (in their cause or correction) they are inevitably interrelated with a persons spiritual beliefs and spiritual state. Emotional wholeness is directly related to Christlikeness.

- A crucial and integrating factor in achieving healing and wholeness is a personal relationship with Jesus Christ. It should be obvious that wholeness is not possible apart from Jesus Christ.

- Healthy relationships are the linchpins of mental, emotional and spiritual health. The Bible teaches directly and gives numerous examples for us to learn from. The Bible covers such issues as personal hygiene, diet, exercise, relationships, parenting, which encompass the human 'psyche' therefore much pastoral counsel and advice is by nature psychological.

- Healing of the mind, emotions and spirit is possible.

- The goal of Biblical counselling is not happiness, but Christlikeness – this theme is developed later.

Healing and wholeness will not come, or last without sound Biblical teaching and obedience to the Word and will of God.

I don't think any of us would have any qualms about that kind of Biblical counselling. It has to be acknowledged that over the years there have been groups and help programmes which have claimed to be Christian, and have used the Bible and Christian terminology to 'package' their ideas, which under closer examination have been considerably less than Biblical and sometimes no different at all to secular approaches.

If we were to take a step back from the debate as it has been, we can first of all notice that all people have a 'psychology' in the same way that C.S. Lewis observed that all people have a theology – thoughts about God which affect their behaviour – so too we have our own thoughts on why people do what they do. We may not call those thoughts our 'psychological theory' but that is what they are. With our theology we can choose to hold on to our old beliefs, and resist any new information, resulting in a poor and inaccurate view of God – this is not what God would want. We are also able to choose to do the same with our beliefs and understanding of human psychology, I do not believe that would serve us any better.

Josh McDowell states, 'The acknowledgement of valuable psychological research and techniques do not compromise the fact that ultimate healing and wholeness comes from God through Christ, any more than consulting a physician betrays a lack of faith in God's sovereign love and ability.' There are few Christians that would deny that God is able to use and work through the skill and insight of a medical doctor, in fact medical work has been one of the great vehicles for missionary endeavour. A similar thought carries over into the mental and emotional domain. There is a parallel between the health and hygiene requirements in Leviticus and Exodus, to the many insights of Hebraic psychology found in Psalms and Proverbs, concerning the heart, mind, emotions and behaviour.

Another consideration is whether we honour God by ignoring technology and progress – where would be the testimony in performing surgery with a butter knife, when the world is wielding a scalpel? Surely we would do well to use and be the best of what is available. As we look at the highest intention of both sides of the debate we actually find agreement – those using psychology want the will of God (Christlikeness) actualised in peoples lives and will use appropriate means to accomplish that end. Those *seemingly* opposed to psychology also want the will of God (Christlikeness) actualised in peoples lives, and are rightly concerned that only appropriate means are used, and that glory and credit goes to where it is due (God). Jay Adams says, 'Methodology and technique, skill and exercise of gifts are all consonant with the work of the Spirit. What makes the difference is ones attitude and inner motivation: does he do what he does in reliance upon his own efforts, in dependence upon methods and techniques, or does he acknowledge his own inability, and ask the Spirit to use his gifts and methods?'

We face real and often painfully messy problems that need real and effective solutions. Think of the breakdown of a marriage relationship. Churches have often handled this badly, with solutions ranging from ignoring (and even ostracising) the couple, to mediation, prayer, teaching, even 'prophetic insight' to find where the sin really came from – I question whether any of these is enough in their own right (except the first one, which is too much!). It is easy to see that we run no risk of self reliance if we have no skills or techniques; we would also run no risk of helping other people to know the love and compassion of God available through Biblical counselling either – I'm sure that you, like me, want to master the art of loving.

The Way ahead

NeuroLinguistic Programming (NLP) is not an invention, it is not a psychology, rather it is a discovery. It is no more created than gravity is, Newton did not create gravity but rather noticed how God had worked in the universe. We too can benefit from a knowledge of what God has placed in front of us, especially what is revealed in the Bible.

NLP is a neutral set of tools, **neurology** refers to our body and brain, these can be used either for sin or for righteousness. Rom 6.12-14 shows us we have a choice to make as to how we will direct our body, but a body itself is neither morally good or bad but how we use it makes the difference. **Language** (the linguistic part) is neutral also. James tells us in his letter that the tongue (and the words we speak) can either bless or curse, build up or tear down (Ch 3.2-12). By **'programming'** we mean the patterns of behaviour, much like a computer programme will run and access the same system resources to accomplish the same results. It also gives us a useable metaphor to understand how to intervene and 'upgrade' out-of-date programmes. We all know from our own experience that habits can be good and are most noticeable when they are bad, but the ability to have habits is part of the way God has designed humanity. Jesus went to the synagogue 'as was his custom'. He also said Pharisees always stoned the prophets. The 'founders' of NLP did not design a system or theory – they simply worked with people and found out some of the principles of human experience.

With NLP modelling skills, you can become a better Christian by focusing on how Jesus used his neurology, language and his habitual patterns. You can, however, become a better Pharisee, a better hypocrite, or even a better Buddhist! The modelling tools themselves do not determine the subject of our modelling any more than the scalpel can decide if it will cut to heal or to hurt. Our bodies, language and habits need direction as we renew our minds according to the truth of the Bible. It is the decisions that we make about what we will model that are good or bad; the modelling process itself is neutral. Our will is important in this, it is like a magnifying glass lens, we put it under the Sun's rays to collect and focus them into one beam so we can start a fire. We all know that the strength is not in the lens but in the Solar beam! Our will is only powerful for change when directed toward the truth, we are not dealing with willpower and positive affirmations, but a decision to 'Fix our eyes on Jesus' (Heb 12.2), get on with the race, and help any others whose path crosses ours (read Lk 10.25-37).

Human needs

Many Christians accept what psychologists and sociologists have developed concerning the needs that we have as human beings, and how we are motivated towards their fulfilment. The Bible shows that we were created with needs, and that needs themselves are not wrong, bad or sinful. However, since the Fall we have often gone about meeting them in selfish or self pleasing ways that have been at other peoples' expense. Jesus, who is fully human had needs but went about meeting them in sinless ways, which helps us twofold, first by knowing it can be done, and second, by giving us many specific examples we can model.

Dr Derek Copley[2] looks at the first few chapters of Genesis and highlights the pre-fall needs of Adam and Eve as: *Purpose* – God gave them a job to do, to rule, tend, keep and to fill the earth (Gen 1.27-30), man also has the needs for *belonging, loving* and *being loved* – as God looked at His creation the only thing that was not good was that man was alone, as humans we have a need to have relationships with God and with each other (Gen 2.18). We also have the needs of *significance* and *'self-esteem'*, these come from our value in being created in the image of God, our relating to Him and others, and also how well we relate to our purpose or mission (Gen 1.26-28, 2.25). With Jesus as our model we can see how each of these needs can be met legitimately. Jesus was truly a 'man with a mission', and He relied on His relationship with God the Father so he was 'independent of His circumstances' (see Heb 12.2, John 6.15, Phil 4.11-13). We are more familiar with seeing inappropriate attempts at meeting needs, for example the need for purpose in our culture has distorted towards materialism and a compulsive urge to 'get things', or 'to be on top'; belonging gone wrong is the unthinking herd mentality (remember the so-called 'Gadarene swine' principle: just because the group are moving in formation and in the same direction, it doesn't mean they are right); love has been mistaken for sexual promiscuity, and the most pervasive are significance and esteem, where we find that inner and outer criticism, manipulation and power-plays to bolster poor self esteem, which essentially says 'if I tear you down and stand on you, I will feel taller'. Because God has made us with needs, there are plenty of healthy ways to meet them; if we go about it in wrong or sinful ways, it is like drinking salt water, it doesn't satisfy and eventually makes you sick!

A more well-known scheme of understanding needs is that of Abraham Maslow. He drew a triangle which represented a hierarchy of needs, which at the base has physiological needs – the needs of food, drink, rest, clothing, shelter, our most basic, bottom-line needs. The next chunk up is safety and security needs, that assuming that we are alive, our next level of concern is staying that way – this functions as a hierarchy because if we have extreme physiological needs, i.e. food, we will forego safety until that need is met (this pattern follows all the way up the triangle). Often this need is expressed in feeling threatened, anxious or fearful. Higher than these then are our love and affection needs, which if unmet feel like loneliness, lack of appreciation, rejection, dejection and isolation. Above that on the triangle are self esteem needs; if these are unmet they express themselves as feelings of guilt, failure, inadequacy, and embarrassment. Finally the 'highest' level of need (which is only ever an issue if the lower levels are at least partly met) is that of 'self actualisation', unmet this would feel like frustration, emptiness, uselessness, boredom and lack of fulfilment. I believe that each of these needs are opportunities for the church to serve and be good news, if we have eyes to see what is in front of us. General Booth said that you couldn't preach the gospel to a man with an empty stomach – can you see how that fits into this scheme yet? Similarly to offer a soup kitchen in some of the more prosperous parts of the world would completely miss the needs and opportunities. If we address the guilt, emptiness, boredom and feelings of inadequacy felt in postmodern cultures, we can open the door for the saving and healing power of God.

The last angle I would like to take on our needs has been developed by Tony Robbins. He sees that many tensions people have are caused by the paradox of needs: we have a need for certainty – to feel certain we can avoid pain and stress and gain pleasure. This can be met in consistency or habit (even down to eating the same fast food products because you know what you are getting!). The paradox clicks in with need number two: we also need uncertainty or variety, we get bored and stagnate if we have too much certainty, so we like surprise, differences and challenge – but not too much! If we have more than we can cope with we become stressed, and retreat into 'security'. Possible for vehicles for meeting this need are a new job, learning something new or having an affair! Again it is worth repeating, the needs are not wrong, but some of the ways we think we can fulfil them are. The next paradox is that of significance and affection and love, according to Robbins. We feel significance by feeling needed or a sense of purpose or uniqueness, but also want to share this with someone (the need of love and acceptance) and so we start to bond with someone, have a sense of oneness and intimacy, but too much of this and 'significance' clicks in and says 'if we are one, then who am I?' and then (sometimes) will act in 'unique' ways that drive people away. Involvement in street gangs could be an example of the need for connection, and armed robbery an example of significance – at least in the victim's eyes! (An interesting observation that John Gray makes in *Men are from Mars*, is that men seem to have a lower threshold for intimacy and will 'pull away' for a short time to rediscover themselves, whereas women are able to maintain closeness for much longer. Sounds like a recipe for variety and uncertainty!) The last two needs in this scheme are the 'primary, essential and ultimate' needs: for growth and contribution, that as we help others to be fulfilled, we find ourselves growing and being fulfilled too.

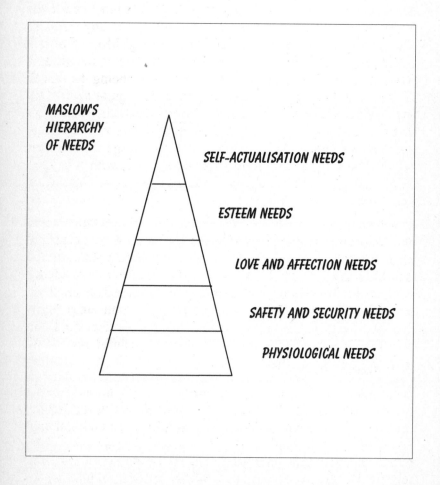

MASLOW'S
HIERARCHY
OF NEEDS

SELF-ACTUALISATION NEEDS

ESTEEM NEEDS

LOVE AND AFFECTION NEEDS

SAFETY AND SECURITY NEEDS

PHYSIOLOGICAL NEEDS

Chapter 3

A Biblical foundation for Change

The Bible is a book of changed lives. You may have your own favourite examples, obvious one that springs to my mind is David who changed from shepherd-boy to King; Moses through the process of time went from a murderer to a leader and prophet; Legions' transformation was from being the local demoniac to having a sound mind, and was a great sign to all who had known him. Now we have started this train of thought, you won't be able to look at your Bible the same way, and you can see that God's will is very much to change us – for the better! The Bible is like a stick of seaside rock with 'Change' running from the first creation to the new creation, Genesis to Revelation.

Change is one of the essentials that we grasp in our relationship with God. The Bible is a book full of changes; first of all there is nothing and chaos, then God speaks and there is creation and order, that's a fairly major change don't you think? what about the change that took place when Adam and Eve sinned? Again this was of cosmic proportions. You can see now why we are in a position where God being perfect does not change (Malachi 3.6) and therefore we, being sinful, need to!

God never changes

The Bible never asks or answers the question 'is there a God?', but starts in Genesis 1 with the statement of fact 'In the beginning God …' The whole Bible, the whole of Christianity, or any of the worlds religions for that matter, and also our own individual and personal understandings of the universe and life, become a nonsense if you take God out of them. Subjectively, the vast majority of people still believe there is 'a God' usually 'out there', but this is to be expected because God has revealed Himself in a general way to all mankind. What we are seeing in the world today is that in the intense spiritual hunger and search for meaning and security, people are discovering God by a process of elimination – they tried scientific materialism, they tried the pursuit of pleasure or material goods, they even tried the empty deceits of eastern philosophies and religions, and now, exhausted they come back to the true and living God. As they come back, we need to be ready to help and disciple them, to help them learn from what they have been through, but not be hindered by it, and the greatest part is introducing them to the fact the he is a person.

Jesus said in John 17.3 that eternal life is knowing the only true God, not as some impersonal force, or distant creator, but as Father, as Lord. As human beings we are designed to have a relationship with God, to walk with Him and enjoy Him, as we begin to understand some of His characteristics and attributes we become thrilled at how varied and exciting this growing relationship is meant to be, also how this affects our approach to caring, counselling and changing.

God is omnipresent, by this I mean that God is immediately present, He is here NOW, in one sense He is part of all we see and experience, at least potentially – the flip side of this is also that while He can use almost any means to meet us, He is separate, and distinct from what He has made, and is far greater than any concept we can have of Him.

God is not 'very old' as some understand eternality, but rather is outside of time, He is the one who knows the end from the beginning (Rev 21:6), while He can be intimately involved in our experience at a particular time, He is not locked into time passing …

Psalm 90, starting verse 2 says: *Before the mountains were born or you brought forth the earth and the world, from everlasting to everlasting you are God. You turn men back to dust, saying, "Return to dust, O sons of men." For a thousand years in your sight are like a day that has just gone by, or like a watch in the night.* (see also 2 Pet 3.8)

He can review or scan the whole of human history from beginning to end as a person would review yesterday afternoon, or He can focus His attention for the equivalent of a thousand years into just one moment of our experience – it is possible to think of miraculous healing in this sense; that God takes the recovery time and compresses it into a moment.

When God says something, He means it – He doesn't say things just to make us feel good, every word He speaks reflects His character, He is true to His word, when He promises something, He will always follow through and fulfil His promise (Jer 1.12). Most reassuring for us is that He is faithful and committed to us as His people (Rom 8.31-39).

Psalm 103.8 says, *The LORD is compassionate and gracious, slow to anger, abounding in love. He will not always accuse, nor will he harbour his anger for ever; he does not treat us as our sins deserve or repay us according to our iniquities. For as high as the heavens are above the earth, so great is his love for those who fear him; as far as the east is from the west, so far has he removed our transgressions from us. As a father has compassion on his children, so the LORD has compassion on those who fear him; for he knows how we are formed, he remembers that we are dust* (see also Exodus 34.6-7).

Not only does God not give us what we do deserve (punishment) He also gives us what we don't deserve (blessing). This is just a tiny clue to how much He loves and cares for us, and how secure we can be in His grace.

Ex 34.6-7 God is not soft or indulgent, He is completely holy, and to be true to Himself He must punish sin – the question we are faced with is whether we want to try to pay that price ourselves or rely on the work of Jesus where He paid for us as our substitute.

God knows all things, more about you and your circumstances and choices and motivations than you do yourself, He is also all-powerful – He can do all things that do not conflict with His will, and He is in all places, we are never alone – whether we feel alone, or are trying to hide something from Him! See Psalm 139.1-12

God is so wonderful we can't hope to reduce His character and personality down to a few theological terms – knowing Him is the greatest adventure, He never changes, so we can have security and certainty in relating to Him, but He is also greater than any of our thoughts about Him, He is so creative that as we look at just the physical world we can marvel at the variety and design in it all.

Some other things it is useful to hold in our minds when we come to helping people and ourselves in the process of growth and change, is that God created us. He designed us, 'knit us together' (Psalm 139.13), and He knows our makeup and being better than any other. Also, that by nature He is a redeemer, that is, He is able to bring good out of every experience, to broaden our wisdom, to deepen our trust or to equip us with insight and compassion to reach and help others in similar circumstances now (2 Cor 1 vs. 3-4). Finally, we must always remember that God is sovereign, He is in charge, nothing happens without Him knowing and permitting it – not even a sparrow falls to the ground, and we really are worth more than that in His sight. We are able to rely on God's mercy, faithfulness and wisdom because He is able to see the end from the beginning, He is in charge and He says He will complete the work He has begun in us (Phil 1.6)

If God is not going to change then if there is a problem in our relationship it means *we need to change, or be changed.* There are some changes that only God can do, and some that He insists we do – it is the latter where NLP will help.

Because Jesus is fully human, and yet totally pleasing to God, it means there is an 'authentic' human way of living – we have all fallen short of it, but Jesus didn't, He is the real model human, He shows us what life can really be, He shows 'full human potential' because He is not marred or limited by sin, and also because He is fully submitted to His Father, He is as John 5 in the Message says 'Aligned with the Father' – where every part of himself was pulling in the same direction as God.

Jesus is the head of a new humanity, a new species, we are new creations (2 Cor 5.17) and we are more like Jesus than Adam; that means that in Christ we have a different potential to those who don't yet know Him, we really do have unlimited resources, we really can 'live it up!' in the full and abundant life He wants for us (John 10.10).

Change is at the heart of God's dealings with humanity. One thing that is universal in our human experience, whether Christian or not, is that we want to change something, it's easy for us to say that we want to change our environment, or things we have, and then we would be happy – but then, do you know people who have those things who are unhappy, even if they have all you ever wanted?

It is not the conditions of our lives that we really need to change, although obviously, when you can , they might help, but rather we need to be able to change two things: firstly how we *feel*, and secondly how we *behave*, or the things we do. Can you think of something you want to change? Why do you want to change that? Is it so you will *feel* happy and in control? If we follow the train of thought far enough, it is almost always the case.

Change is one of the essentials that we grasp in our relationship with God, the Bible is a book full of changes; first of all there is nothing and chaos, then God speaks and there is creation and order thats a fairly major change don't you think? what about the change that took place when Adam and Eve sinned? again this was of cosmic proportions, you can see now why we are in a position where God being perfect does not change (Malachi 3.6) and therefore we being sinful need to!

One small thing I should mention here that will prevent confusion later on is that *happiness is a by-product, not a goal*. Larry Crabb[3] puts it like this 'Many of us place top priority not on becoming Christlike in the middle of our problems, but on finding happiness. Now there is nothing wrong in wanting to be happy. An obsessive preoccupation with "my happiness", however, often obscures our understanding of the biblical route to deep, abiding joy. I want to be happy but the paradoxical truth is that I will never be happy if I am primarily concerned with becoming happy. My overriding goal must be in every circumstance to respond biblically, to put the Lord first, to seek to behave as He would want me to. The wonderful truth is that as we devote all our energies to the task of becoming what Christ wants us to be, He fills us with joy unspeakable and a peace far surpassing what the world offers ... I must firmly and consciously by an act of my will reject the goal of becoming happy and adopt the goal of becoming more like the Lord. The result will be happiness for me' (p.15).

'Biblical anthropology'

Volumes have been written on the nature of man, from the standpoints of philosophy, theology and the sciences. It is not my intention to try to answer some of the 'big questions' that have baffled more able minds, but rather to continue to lay a foundation that gives us a workable platform to operate from. We must have Biblical view of man, which means, if God made us (and He did) we must take His word on our make-up, needs and motivations. This does not discount the sciences or philosophy, it just ensures that we interpret them correctly, we take the eternal word and interpret the latest research and thinking according to that which doesn't change. How many times have we seen the church 'buy into' a secular way of thinking, compromise its stand on the truth, and then find that science or whatever then 'discovers' something else which vindicates the Bible, by which time Christians are feeling confused and adrift.

Some of the pervading views that we can see in postmodern society are that man is a highly evolved animal, but he is only an animal, all 'higher functions' are only physical and chemical, that 'love' is only a biochemical and hormonal storm, and truth is subjective. Another erroneous view would say that we are really spirits who inhabit the physical realm, that we may have existed before (i.e. reincarnation) and that the physical realm is not important at all, we are 'above' morality. We can see these views reflected in 'scientific materialism', 'secular humanism' and 'animism'. Even Paul in New Testament times was trying to correct a worldview which said 'the spirit is everything, the body is nothing' and although as a generalisation, Western culture has it completely the other way round (the body is everything, the spirit is nothing) some of Paul's teaching still applies. In Athens (Acts 17, and all of 1 Corinthians) Paul teaches that the body is not a prison either to ignore (like in ascetic practices) or to indulge (in debauchery, etc.), but is rather a temple for God to live in (1 Cor 6.19-20). The body is not irrelevant (1 Tim 4.8), nor is it everything (1 Cor 9.27). The same goes for our spirit or mind, we will not be disembodied in the resurrection, we will have 'spiritual bodies'. Western culture likes to divide things up and compartmentalise them; it is fine to do this to understand individual parts and functions of a person, as long as we put them together again and understand a person in a whole-person way. It is not a question of 'I have a visible part and an invisible part, which is the real me?' – the answer is all of you.

We are made in the image of God, we have been created to reflect God's likeness, in what ways? God is a person, we have personality, God is purposeful and decisive, so are we, God is social – He has relationships, He is moral, He thinks, He remembers, has emotions, so too in our own individual ways we reflect these and many other characteristics. It is interesting to see that God, who is King over all, put man as 'king' of the earth, to subdue it, bring it under his dominion, and to tend it and care for it – man is meant to 'mirror' his Creator. Unfortunately, when Adam sinned, the mirror cracked, and in the Fall the image becomes distorted, it is still there even in the most sad, broken and sinful lives. Through the work of the cross, we are redeemed, it is God's purpose to not only restore the image in us (i.e. to make us Christlike) but to do even more than that, we are now joined to God in the spirit (1 Cor 6.17) and are showing *that* family likeness! (see 1 John 3.1-3, Eph 4.23-24)

Having laboured the point sufficiently we can now look at some of the individual characteristics that make up this wonderful creature called humanity, with an understanding that we are not really divided into watertight compartments. We all have a physical body. The Bible says a lot about our bodies, ranging from our formation in the womb (Ps 139.13), through various food or washing laws in the Old Testament and via miracles of healing, to our future resurrection bodies. We have bodies which we live in and are owned by God (1 Cor 6.17-20). We are more than just bodies, we are also intellectual or mental creatures, that is we have a thought life, we think, worry, plan, scheme and are also able to choose and decide. If that weren't enough we are also emotional beings, we feel joy, sorrow, fear, hope, pride, love, and also pleasure and pain – these affect our bodies and our thoughts more than we may like to admit. Finally we are also spiritual, we are able to have a relationship with God, and others that is beyond physical, intellectual and emotional bonds, and again the spiritual dimension affects all other areas of our experience – we are all these things all at once, and we are truly 'fearfully and wonderfully made!' (Psalm 139) One other dimension which is too frequently overlooked is that we are social beings, we have been designed to relate to God, and to each other, and our thoughts, words and actions do not only affect our experience, but alter and shape the lives of people around us, not only immediately, but through time as well, one of the weaknesses of the twentieth century is blindness to our community and consequences in our world. Dr Michael D. Yapko said, 'I think that the emphasis on personal freedom at the expense of social responsibility has been the biggest mistake we have made in our culture'.

We will seldom have people come in to see us and complain that life is going too well for them, it is often pain of some kind that is the motivator for change. There are several levels of 'problems' to consider. Firstly we are aware of physical difficulties. If you were to picture Maslow's triangle you would see that many of the problems that force their way into our consciousness as most urgent will be physical. I say urgent, and not important, because there are times when we can do something painful or dangerous because it is 'right' or for a higher motive like love. We can 'override' the physical level by changing the meanings to do something important (see section on Christian Life Reframing). Similarly, how often do we get caught up with the 'urgent' which is not important? Physical problems can present themselves in several ways (apart from just the ageing process, which is a science in its own right) for example an *accident*, when something happens to us, from simply stubbing our toe to having to be cut from a car wreck, accidents certainly do happen. Then there is the area of *disease* or sickness, which could cover things like viruses or bacteria that affect our bodies functioning and cause pain. Beyond that there are *hereditary* or genetic difficulties – we inherit more than just our good looks from our parents and grandparents;

sometimes we get some of their weaknesses too. Of course there is our *lifestyle*, it has been said that our culture is 'digging its grave with its teeth', it's obvious that habitual drug, alcohol and tobacco abuse will take their toll in our physical bodies, less obvious but equally powerful are the ways we use and abuse food, poor hygiene, sexual promiscuity, lack of sleep, a sedentary lifestyle with little or no exercise and general self neglect. Finally *psychosomatic*, in the body we would think of this as dis-ease, that because of the wonderful mind-body, body-mind we have been given, our thoughts can cause real problems (or benefits). Just because something starts in someone's mind, doesn't mean it isn't real or will stay 'just in their head'!

Because much of this book is going to be giving specific strategies and tools to renew and transform our thinking-feeling, we can simply say at this stage that most of the unpleasant or disempowering feelings found in unmet needs on Maslow's Triangle come into the category of mental and emotional problems, from stress, breakdowns, depression, anxiety, paranoia, schizophrenia and phobias to the more general malaise of aimlessness and confusion. Interestingly, as we read a list like that, to make sense of it we either picture one of those states in our mind's eye, or tell ourselves something about it, and then give those representations feeling in our bodies – we are fearfully and wonderfully made, are we not?

Sometimes 'at the back of' problems we find another invisible source or dimension, which is why as Christians we should not only be precise in our 'diagnosis' but also exercise our discernment, this comes as we are open to God's 'inklings' and are well grounded in the truth (Heb 5.14) The spiritual realm is also divided into several spheres, the *human spirit* has a primary need to be regenerated and know God, but also there are references to a troubled spirit (Gen 41.8, Dan 2.1, Jn 13.21, Dan 7.15 etc.) a fainting or overwhelmed spirit (Ps 142.3, 143.4,7) a grieved spirit (Isa 54.6, Prov 12.18,18.21 notice the cause here!) a broken spirit (Prov 18.14, Job 17.1, Prov 15.4,13, Psa 38.8). Another, more well known area would be demonic, for example Luke 9.37-42. Finally, the most important power in the spiritual realm is God's – to draw the lost to Himself, to discipline and restore disobedient Christians (Heb 12.5-11) and sometimes even this discipline will involve the 'innocent' (Abimilech Gen 20.17-18)

Although Christians and not-yet Christians alike would like to duck this one, the Bible says that there are definitely consequences to our actions, whether as profound as where we will spend eternity, to the more immediate consequences of last night's Vindaloo! Galatians 6.5-6 states that God is not mocked, a man will reap what He sows, fortunately this is a two-way street that is travelled by God's mercy too, but if we sow to the flesh we will reap a bitter harvest (Rom 8.13) and if we sow righteousness and peace we will reap the fruit of the Spirit (Gal 5.22-23).

Let's have a look at some of the *levels or dimensions of change*, this section is a transcript of a training I did in 1996:

> First, there is the level of *beliefs*, now I want to break this into two kinds, firstly, 'theological' beliefs, which are what we believe about God, man, sin, etc., the most important of which is that a person believes in Jesus as Lord and Saviour (without this belief and the consequence of having a living relationship with God through Him, all other change is simply rearranging the pictures in a burning house!). Or again one might say "I believe God heals" this will very much determine this ones behaviour in that he will (if he is consistent) pray for the sick, and if you didn't believe it, why waste your time and God's asking Him to?

> You see, beliefs control what we will even consider possible, what we will see and experience of the world – how many of you can look back with hindsight and see that God was working in your life before you were saved? Aha! but you didn't notice at the time did you? Why is that? Because you had a belief that said 'there is no God', therefore you couldn't allow yourself to see Him!

> The other kind of beliefs are 'life' beliefs, these are just beliefs that you pick up that are more general. I remember working with a girl who had been anorexic for many years, and she *believed* that her body was disgusting, she just 'knew' that when anything went

wrong it was her fault! How about that for having beliefs that will cause you pain in life?

Of course in the real world, theological and 'life' beliefs are intertwined. What about Sarah, for example (Gen. 18.1-15), she had a belief in that she 'knew' that old ladies don't have babies, of course they don't! Right? No, God gives her a new belief 'is anything too hard for the Lord?' which opens up a new possibility. She and Abraham both need to apply action to the new belief and hey presto! Isaac is born, what a laugh it can be to have a new belief about Gods power *now!*

A part of what God does with us in bringing us to maturity in Christ is replacing our old 'life' beliefs with eternally true 'theological' beliefs from his word, and suddenly a whole new world of possibility opens up.

Another area we can see change is in *values*. Paul writes in Phil 3.7-8 that his old values of being a top-notch Jew and Pharisee were as dung and refuse in the light of knowing Christ. Many of us have had our values turned upside down, whether that be in the realm of right and wrong, or in what we think is important or not. When one of your friends is mad keen on stamp collecting and you think that is no big deal, what is that a difference of? Yes, values. We can discover our values just by asking about any particular area of life 'what's important to me about ...?'. Your answers to those questions, about life, relationships, family, money, spirituality and so on will give you a good idea of what kinds of things you would enjoy and what kinds of things would bring you real pain.

Then there is the high level change in *identity*. I suppose the obvious one is Saul to Paul. Identity is the set of beliefs you have about yourself, who you are, how you define yourself. What would you read as a definition if you looked up your name in the dictionary? What makes you different from the fellow sitting next to you? These are all parts of your identity. Interestingly, as a belief it can limit our behaviours in both positive and negative ways, for example, if you asked me to dress in a tutu and run down the high street shouting 'the queen is a man' I would turn you down, because 'I'm not like that – that's not the kind of person I am.' This can be a very positive thing, it prevents me from unhelpful behaviours, but also because my identity is as a Christian, I will do things that are even uncomfortable for me to do, reaching out to people who are in desperate need, dying or in pain, and also not doing things that the Bible teaches as sinful. If you have an identity as 'a loser', will that affect the way you approach life than if you perceive yourself as 'a child of God'? Try this one on for size—a Charlie Brown cartoon based on 'all the world's a stage': Charlie is talking to Linus and says, "I stepped out onto the stage of life, and a voice called out 'No, he's wrong for the part!' "

We can change our *behaviour*, Eph 4.22-24 instructs us to put off, be renewed in the spirit of our minds, and then put on better behaviour, holy, righteous and consistent with our new identity as God's new creation. Notice that this isn't just remedial, in terms of just stopping sinning, but more so in terms of growing into Christlikeness and maturity in the Spirit. God doesn't change, we have to, He is the rock, He is perfect that means there is no flaw in him to get worse, or to improve. Our experience of Him changes because He is infinite, and we encounter new facets of Him, this is part of the adventure that Heaven will be. Change is a major issue in the Christian life.

The last level of change I want to mention is that of changing our thinking or *changing our mind*, and the Bible has plenty to say about it explicitly, but also was of course written so God could reveal Himself to us, so we would change the way we think, that is why the Bible is the most important reference book we have in thinking about change. All lasting change must bring us more closely into line with God's Word and with what He says about life, behaviour and what is important and what things mean; if we don't we are deceiving ourselves and going down a blind alley. Repentance, the word is meta-noia, means changing your mind. An example from the Bible is in Acts 3.19

what did they need to repent from? they had crucified Christ, God had raised him from the dead and made him Lord of all, and were they in trouble! They needed to change their thinking about Jesus and turn to God! Quite often this is an emotional event as well, these people were cut to the heart, that is because we often need a bit of pain to shift our old habitual thought patterns.

Rom 12.2 says, *'Do not be conformed to this world but be transformed by the renewing of your mind so that you may know what is that good and perfect and acceptable will of God'*

A helpful way of summarising all this is in Robert Dilts' *Logical Levels of Personality* (1990), which helps us pinpoint where a problem is presenting itself, as well as where we would need to make a change. Notice the impact that each of these levels has on you if you pretend that you were a child who had done poorly on an exam:

Level 1) *environment*	The teacher says 'it's not your fault; there were builders noises and distractions in the classroom'. This has little impact at all, the problem was outside of you, and so the changes to make would involve going somewhere else, changing your surroundings. So Level 1 deals with external constraints, and asks the questions 'where were you?' 'when or what else was happening outside of you?'
Level 2) *behaviours*	The teacher could focus on our specific behaviour and say, 'You did poorly on that test'. That gives the responsibility to us, for our actions (or lack of them) So Level 2 is about the quality of our operation on environment what did you do?

Level 3) capabilities	Our teacher now begins to 'chunk up' the levels of abstraction as she says something like 'you are not very good at this kind of school work' or 'you are not very good at numbers', this has much wider implications and deeper impact. Level 3 takes notice of our 'maps' and strategies, and asks 'how?'
Level 4) belief and value systems	If the teacher said 'that test is not important, it's only important that you enjoy learning' she would be stating the values she holds (and reinforcing the belief that the grade isn't as important as the learning process) Level 4 asks 'why?'
Level 5) identity	If the teacher said 'you are stupid' or 'you do not try' or 'you are no good' her statements touch the whole being, the core, and the impact is pervasive Level 5) deals with the 'spiritual' and asks 'who?'

This model is not only useful for diagnosing a problem, but helps us view the Bible in an interesting way; a level can be changed not only by intervention on that level (like changing to a quieter room) but also on any of the levels above, e.g. if I acquired the capability to concentrate in any environment, it will affect my behaviour and the way I relate to my environment (distraction). Look again at the section 'dimensions of change' and see how many examples there are of God intervening at a higher logical level and 'outframing' a problem, for example Paul. God did not intervene directly on his behaviour of persecution, but changed his identity, which changed his beliefs, values, capabilities and this produced completely opposite behaviours. We will learn how to do this for ourselves and others.

There is a direction for real and lasting change, that draws us closer to objective reality as revealed in the unchanging Word of God, of course there are many other directions, which deny truth, which produce phoney change, which ultimately costs so much more, but we are interested in the kind of transformation that leads us to be all that God intends for us.

Hands on

- What are the verses and concepts that you use most when faced with a problem? or when someone asks you for help?

- Look at the list of God's characteristics and for each one complete this sentence 'Because God is X, I can (am, can no longer, will) Y

- Discuss with a friend 'if God's plan for us is ongoing change, why are (personal and church) rituals and traditions so attractive to many people?'

- Read a newspaper or magazine, what concepts of man do they promote, reread some articles asking 'what needs are being met by this persons comments / behaviour?'

- Watch TV, what 'causes' are most commonly attributed to natural disasters? wars? Individual violent crime?

- Listen in conversation for statements from different 'logical levels': environment (where? when?), behaviours (what?) capability (how?) beliefs and values (why?) and identity (who?).

Chapter 4

The Values of Christian Change-work

As you look around the world you will see lots of people offering 'quick fix' feel- good approaches to life. Most of them have positive intentions to help people, some of them have useful ideas and skills, but there is a problem. The 'personal development' movement or the human potential movement can't deliver the goods for the whole person, it is not a matter of positive thinking if most of the world are separated from God, but rather positive action by Gods people, bringing the truth and the power of God to bear in peoples lives NOW. Even the best psychologies and technologies are useless unless in the greater context of God's Kingdom and the redemption He has provided. So what are some of the things that make Christian change-work unique? well for a start, our values …

When we think about changing ourselves or helping others, the values are the 'priority context'; they remind us what is important, in not only what results we aim for, but also the means we will use. Think back to the logical levels, can you remember a time when you wanted to help someone, when your specific behaviour 'failed' yet because you functioned from the higher level value of 'love' or 'respect', there was still a positive outcome? Here some of the values, beliefs and goals in Christian change-work.

1) **God wants us whole**. Hopefully by now we are familiar with the fact that what God wants is for us to be constantly moving towards Christlikeness, and showing the life on the inside more and more on the outside. Of all the people we can ever think of, Jesus is the most whole and 'together' person, and He is of course, the second Adam, the head of a

renewed humanity. Way back in Genesis, we read about Adam being formed from the dust of the ground (ch. 2 v 7), and later in chapter 3 how not just Adam, but the whole creation was cursed and started to become deformed as a result of sin and the reign of death, then through the redemptive work of Christ on the cross in history, and the Holy Spirits' ongoing application of that work in our lives today. Think about it: we are to be transformed into an even greater creation than the original.

- *Wholeness demonstrated in Jesus' ministry.* Jesus stated that His ministry was empowered by the Spirit to preach the gospel to the poor, heal the brokenhearted, proclaim liberty to captives, recovery of sight to the blind, to set free the oppressed and to proclaim the acceptable year of the Lord (Luke 4.18-19). The rest of His ministry was taken up with a) teaching people so they had a correct understanding and healthy faith in God, b) developing the characters of His disciples so they could continue His ministry, realising their potential in God, c) healing the sick, cleansing lepers, freeing the demonised, forgiving the sinner, raising the dead, etc. Jesus stated that He never did anything or said anything except under the guidance of His Father (John 5.19-20), therefore we can know that it is God's will that these people be made whole, and Jesus is the same, yesterday, today and forever (Heb 13.8) so He still wants us whole. See how 'holistic' Jesus' ministry was, and is, covering the whole person and also personal relationships, 'social' wholeness and integration too.

- *Wholeness demonstrated in the work of Redemption.* When we look beyond the earthly ministry of Jesus it becomes even more apparent that God wants us whole, as the work of Calvary in redeeming us and making us righteous firstly qualifies us to be indwelt by the Holy Spirit, but allows us to be those who 'taste of the powers of the age to come' – that is when the image is completely restored, when there is no more pain, crying, death, sorrow etc. (Rev 21.4). If the end results of the Redemption are wholeness, holiness and freedom from sickness or pain, again it becomes obvious that God wants us whole.

- *Wholeness in John 10.10.* while some people have taken this verse to mean much more than Jesus meant by it, the Greek suggests an abundant, overflowing, fullness of life that is at very least the opposite of what we had when we were under the sway of Satan, so we have God giving freely to us, giving life to us and causing us to be fruitful and established.

— *Wholeness comes from relating correctly with God*. There is no real wholeness that is apart from God, or teaches us to live contrary to His nature. There have been times in all our lives when it felt as though we were working 'across the grain' of life, that is because God has set in place both natural, spiritual and moral laws in the universe, which we ignore at our peril. We do well to remember this because we cannot break His spiritual laws any more than we really can His natural laws, if you were to jump off a tall building, you would not break the law of gravity, but it would certainly break you! Similarly with personal integrity, sin, honesty, etc., we must know there is a high price that is paid in our lives and those who we seek to help, in trying to do things our way. Jesus taught in Matt 6.33 we should put first things first. Someone once said 'if God is not Lord of all, He is not Lord at all', we need to know who has the first word and the last word in our lives, and this is best decided upon **before** a crisis hits. When I was a child my mother taught me to do my collar shirt button up first, as then the rest of the buttons would hang correctly and would not get muddles – if I started in the middle I would often find I had a 'spare' button at the top or bottom. So it is with God. He said that if we seek Him first, with His righteousness and Lordship, then all the other things would 'line up right'. If we misunderstand this then all other change will be impotent, as we will be helping people to live as rebels, independent of God.

Jerry White of the Navigators said, 'God, the Word of God and the souls of men, according to the Bible these are the only three things that last to eternity, and to the extent that we are involved in these, we are involved in eternity'. It is so good not to have to be tied into just this present moment, but rather to be able to step back and view our circumstances and changes in the light of eternity. When we recall what does last and what does not, it will help us to hold on to the really important things and let go of the temporary and often urgent things.

2 Cor 4.16-18 *Therefore we do not lose heart. Though outwardly we are wasting away, yet inwardly we are being renewed day by day. For our light and momentary troubles are achieving for us an eternal glory that far outweighs them all. So we fix our eyes not on what is seen, but on what is unseen. For what is seen is temporary, but what is unseen is eternal.*

2) **All change should bring us closer to Him.** By the time you have completed this book you will know just how easy it is to make someone 'feel better' or happy, but if any changes take us away from reality as it is, by blotting out or distorting unpleasantness, then it will not last and is deceptive, and takes us away from genuine growth. The apostle Paul had been responsible for persecuting the church, he was more than happy to be forgiven and leave it behind him, but we nowhere see him denying it ever happened at all.

3) **God has eternal priorities** In the account of the healing of the paralytic man in Mk 2 we can observe that Jesus was more concerned about the intangible part of this man, his spirit, soul and his relationship to God. This is expressed in Jesus not immediately meeting the felt need of healing for his legs, but addressing the problem of his sin and guilt. A second principle is that Jesus used his immobility as an opportunity to get him right with God, if He had healed him first, there would have been the chance that he would not be aware of his greater need and would be able to 'walk to hell'. One thing I often discuss with people who come to see me is how to use their new freedom or abilities in godly ways that draw them closer to God, rather than having got what they want from God, now pleasing themselves and not Him.

Other thoughts that are helpful to have in our minds relate to

– *The New Creation.* Read 2 Cor 5.17, if we are to truly take God at His word then this is one of the most liberating truths for us, we are born of God, we are part of the new humanity with Jesus as our second Adam, a whole new species, if you like, and the old things that had us bound, downtrodden and defeated are passed away, and all things, ALL THINGS have become new! Realise that the person you are helping is someone for whom Jesus Christ gave His life. Part of our role is to teach people what God says, as the entrance of His word brings light (Ps 119.130), and faith comes by hearing the word (Rom 10.17) and praying for a revelation of that truth which will bring a change in thinking and behaviour. *We cannot rely too heavily on the Word of God.*

- *the indwelling Holy Spirit.* We have treasure in clay jars, people who come to us are not after us, but the treasure, we have to rely on the power of the Holy Spirit which is in us (Eph 1.19ff), knowing He can do immeasurably more than we can ask or imagine (Eph 3.20), we also rely on His wisdom and not on our own (Prov 3.5-6) and actively seek to be led by Him, through our knowledge of scripture, also through thoughts, words, pictures, impressions, hunches, 'inklings', etc., where He may reveal to us the keys to a problem. We count on the fact of the Holy Spirit working through us and in the other person, He is the 'Senior Counsellor' in the room!.

- *Sin and independence from God.* Billy Graham is reported to have said the around 95% of Christians in our day are 'carnal' in the sense of 1 Cor 3.1-3, with unconfessed sin in their lives, therefore short-circuiting the power of God, and having to act like 'mere men' – relying upon their own strength and resourcefulness (and cunning!) to get by. Sin is simply the greatest source of defeat and problems in the world, we isolate ourselves from God, and often, as believers, also experience conviction and the loving discipline of God designed to wake us up! (Heb 12.5ff) Keep in mind that your 'client' is a sinner. To be restored to God is as simple as confessing our sin to Him as taught in 1 John 1.9. Confession involves agreeing that what we did is sin, agreeing that Christ died on the cross to provide forgiveness and freedom from that sin, agreeing and receiving that forgiveness. We will discuss repentance and being filled with the Holy Spirit later.

- *Repentance.* What we are open to will affect us, and repentance is like a revolving door that determines what we are open to, for example; we can be open to our past, and find ourselves affected by it in terms of feelings of pain, overwhelm, depression and sadness; we can be open to our self consciousness now, this can affect how we engage with others, whether we appear to be self absorbed, not listening or interested. Being open to self in this way also can bring out some factors like pride, where perhaps we will not enter into praise and worship because we are to conscious of our shortcomings, or how we will appear to others. Repentance is the act of turning fully away from all, and turning fully towards God, as we are open to Him, He pours in His healing, we put our past behind us, we put aside the sin which so easily besets, we put our pride beneath our feet (see Phil 3.13-14, and, 1Thess 1.9). There are some areas of a person's life which will not change if they refuse to repent. As we confess our sin, we also repent of it, allowing God to direct us, and not our passions, we turn away from it and look to God for the grace and strength to help in our time of need (Heb 4.16).

- *(Un)forgiveness.* In my experience of pastoral work, one of the biggest issues in the area of sin and repentance is unforgiveness. In the Lord's Prayer we are taught to ask 'forgive us our sins AS WE FORGIVE them that have sinned against us', while in eternity we are qualified for heaven (Col 1.13) and made perfect (Heb 10.14) with our sins past, present and future covered by the work of Jesus, our experience of that forgiveness in this life is conditional on us freely forgiving others. We do well to spend time asking about any unresolved relationships, and encouraging people to forgive, ask forgiveness, make restitution where appropriate and to generally seek to be at peace with all men – as much as is possible. If we insist on holding a 'bitter root of unforgiveness' (Heb 12.15) we can be sure it will bear bitter fruit in our lives! Some of the most difficult people you will ever work with are those who are full of bitterness, and those who are too proud to receive forgiveness. Many people find a difficulty in receiving forgiveness, with this it is essential to teach what the word says (for example, 1 Jn 1.9, Ps 103, Rom 8. 38). Maybe even get them to read these scriptures out loud, and to assure them that they are not bigger than God's eternal word, or His faithfulness to his promises.

- *Love.* Hopefully it goes without saying that as Christians we function within the values and framework of love, that we are caring, and seek the good of those around us – any changework we do will seem harsh and manipulative if we are not coming from a place of love. Our need for love is met primarily in God (1 John 4.8) He is love, and loves totally and unconditionally, in comparison to the limited and conditional nature of much of the love we have received from others – there is no self seeking in God's love for us. As we walk with God, and become like Him, we are filled with His Spirit and 'the love of God is shed abroad in our hearts' (Rom 5.5) and we start to love what He loves, in the way that He loves, so our need for love is also met through other believers. Specifically the Bible shows that love provokes to action (it doesn't sit and 'bleat' about the state of the world) love reaches out in an inclusive way, love takes the initiative to heal and restore – God did this in Jesus, and He does it through us (Rom 5.8). Another side of love is that it is totally antagonistic and destructive to the things that are damaging and hurting people, things that prevent them from enjoying what God wants for them (1 Jn 3.8). We hate the sin, guilt and deception that steals the joy and fruitfulness we are intended for. Love never fails (1 Cor 13.8), even when we seem to have got it wrong; if we love and allow God room, there is no failure. This is God's love working through us, it even 'constrains us' (2 Cor 5.16) because it is God's love and is infinite, we can be reckless and extravagant in giving it away, as He will not run out! It is great to have a positive and Christlike compulsion, is it not? At times we feel like saying, 'I'm sorry I'm being tough with you, but my motives are pure.'

– *the Dignity of the individual.* If we perceive someone in a negative way, do you think they pick that up? We may be saying the right things, but it does not 'ring true'. Also, because our perceptions act as filters, we will tend to delete and ignore anything that does not confirm them, so we will only notice things that 'prove' our negative image of others. Some people say 'perception is projection' our internal thoughts affect our bodies, which affect our total communication, and feed back round in ever increasing amounts. We need to develop the ability of seeing as God sees 1 Sam 16.7b 'The LORD does not look at the things man looks at. Man looks at the outward appearance, but the LORD looks at the heart'. This cuts both ways, here: Samuel is not to be impressed by outward strength or beauty, and also not to be put off by what he saw as limitations. Jesus had the ability to be with prostitutes, down and outs, and those who appeared to be the dregs of society, but He easily saw through the dirt, sin and stigma, we can also easily follow in His steps. For a start, we can remember that at one time we were not so great (Eph 2.12-13), but look at the value He put on us: 1 Pt 1.17-19 *'For you know that it was not with perishable things such as silver or gold that you were redeemed from the empty way of life handed down to you from your forefathers, but with the precious blood of Christ, a lamb without blemish or defect.'* We are precious, worthwhile, we are better than just 'OK'. Another thing is to value free will, God created us to be able to choose, and while most of the pain in the world is caused by our wrong choices, God gave us the ability and He will not take it away – Satan however tries to inhibit and limit free will (see 2 Cor 4.4) we cannot do God's work Satan's' way. We are not superior to our 'client' (Phil 2.1-4).

Let's see an example of valuing the dignity of the individual: Jesus and the woman caught in adultery (John 8.1-11). If you can picture in your mind's eye that there is this crowd, with the guilty woman as the focus of attention, how do you think she feels? Terrified, humiliated, exposed and ashamed at very least. Jesus bends down and starts doodling in the sand, the scribes and the Pharisees lean forward to see what He's writing, they ask themselves, 'what is He up to?' – how much attention is on the woman now? Jesus has drawn all the 'heat' from her to Him, He has also broken the mob-rule state of the crowd, and in their momentary confusion, while their hearts are still wide open, He makes the statement that changes the meaning of the whole situation, making the religious people aware of what they had had to ignore to be able to carry on that way (called 'reframing' see later chapter). Why? Because Jesus wanted to give the woman dignity, He drew their attention to Himself, and then demonstrated that the woman was no worse than the scribes, they were equal, AND then He made her better, He forgave her whereas the scribes and Pharisees had gone away feeling guilty and unforgiven, WOW, what a Saviour!

A small example of how I apply this in my Church is that I don't 'demonstrate' when I pray for healing or if I pray with those oppressed by evil spirits – I feel that it puts unhelpful pressure on the individuals, and also could give them a 'label' which might make them uncomfortable in the Church long-term (imagine people saying about you 'Oh, you know the one, they had a 'spirit of pornography and gambling'!). This stops our past becoming part of our identity. I also have used none of the people in my church for the examples you will read later. I know that those who do demonstrate healing do it to stimulate faith and to train others, and in some contexts that is valid, so we must always keep in mind who it is we are helping and serving, and the long term 'ecology' of those decisions.

 – *Abiding in Christ, dwelling in His Body.* many Christians talk about 'Spiritual breathing' by this phrase we mean the process of exhaling the impure – confessing our sin and receiving forgiveness, and inhaling the pure – appropriating the fullness of the Holy Spirit by faith. As we continue to breathe spiritually, we find that God's life and power are unhindered in us, and the fruit of the Spirit becomes more evident in our lives (Gal 5.22-23), and we enjoy the benefits of 'abiding in Christ' John 15.1-7.

   [As we counsel and help people it is useful to see this as one of the most profound concepts to communicate and work towards, that we are to change to permit abiding in Christ, and that with believers every issue is a matter of 'discipleship counselling'.]

If you read John 15, you will notice Jesus teaches us about the relationship we are to have with Him, that the life that has flowed through Him in His earthly ministry, bearing fruit, is to now flow through us. Let's notice a few things of importance from the passage:

It is God the Father who is the one who does the work, ultimately it is not us, we are not to take our spiritual snippers and run amok, lopping off what *we* think should be gotten rid of – so often we are aware of external behaviours, but God is more interested in changing us from the inside out (v.1) We are already clean by the word of forgiveness He has spoken to us (v.3) and it is a natural consequence of abiding in the vine that we are fruitful (v. 4-5,8,16). When a branch has become fruitful it can sometime 'outgrow its strength' and the weight of the fruit pulls the branch down, which can possibly spoil the fruit, or cause a kink in the branch where the sap is 'nipped' and cannot flow freely – the branch now feels dirty, withered, 'burnt out' and unfruitful, all because it was very fruitful! Many of us have experienced this or seen it in the lives of others, so what happens next? God prunes it back (v.2) He lifts it up (v.4 'casts out' is the Greek word *airo*, which means to lift up, compare with 1 Tim 2.8, or should we 'cast off' our hands in worship? This mis-translation has caused many fruitful believers to doubt their salvation) then the Father cleans us up (v.3) and 'straps us' to other believers, the other branches, then we are able to give wisdom and insight to maybe younger and stronger believers as they give support to us until we are stronger ourselves. We are to become fruitful in helping others, but should not counsel if we are going through a rebellious patch.

- *The Body of Christ* is a 'healing thing', one of the gifts God has given the world is the church, we have the truth of the gospel and the power of the Holy Spirit, and on top of that we are a community of God's people who can love. Your 'client' needs other Christians as well as you. We live in a 'dysfunctional world', Aldrich[4], commenting on Maslow's hierarchy of needs says, 'the serving dimension of church life can be expanded if these basic human needs are understood and met ... man's needs are opportunities for us to share God's solution.' See how Christ through His Body can fulfil these needs.

Physiological needs can be met by 'mercy ministry' providing food, drink, rest, health support and shelter. Safety and security needs again can be met as we give peace of mind, assurance and places of sanctuary, refuge and safety. In our fellowship we can address the love and affection needs with companionship, appreciation, acceptance, inclusion and intimacy. Through our teaching and counsel we can help with self esteem needs on issues like forgiveness, confidence, trust, success and recognition. Finally, through an understanding of Gods plan for us, and with an environment of active service, 'self actualisation' needs can be met in purpose, completeness, usefulness, fulfilment and satisfaction. Many churches adopt the use of small groups or kinship groups where discipleship issues are worked out in relationships, where there is social healing and integration, with love and support. The Bible not only gives us the model of Kinships, but also of 'goels', a wise person who we voluntarily submit to, who can advise and help us when we have been given

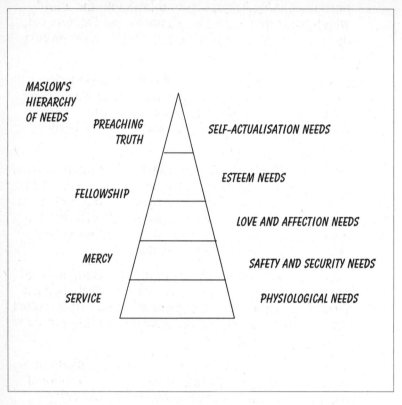

MASLOW'S
HIERARCHY
OF NEEDS

PREACHING TRUTH — SELF-ACTUALISATION NEEDS

ESTEEM NEEDS

FELLOWSHIP — LOVE AND AFFECTION NEEDS

MERCY — SAFETY AND SECURITY NEEDS

SERVICE — PHYSIOLOGICAL NEEDS

too many opinions. The main thing, however, is that in the church we are to have loving relationships, and to work out our relationships in the light of scripture – there is such glorious diversity in the Body of Christ, that God has plenty of ways to help us get our attitudes and character right.

Having an inclusive approach: As Christians we are not in competition with doctors, dentists or qualified professionals; we need to have a cooperative and respectful attitude to those who in the earthly sense have 'our lives in their hands'. Healing can come in quite a few ways, and so we want to be open to as many avenues to help ourselves and others as possible. In his book *The Way* E. Stanley Jones lists eight different vehicles for healing which show a fuller appreciation of our complexity, in the real world. We find an overlap of these in nearly every case:

   Medicine; God has provided many natural cures for
       . alleviating pain and enhancing the bodies healing

process, and He has put natural laws into the world, which when discovered by chemists and Doctors can do the same. If there is a natural ailment, use the cure if it's available!

Surgery; again there are many dedicated and skilled surgeons who, through understanding the way we are made are able to intervene more directly to remove destructive or damaged parts, and allow the body to repair itself.

Nutrition; this is a more powerful factor than many realise, our bodies are incredibly designed, but you can't run a Rolls Royce on beer! When we put into our bodies things which cleanse, nourish and fuel it effectively, many of our systems (as well as our emotions) start to function the way they were created.

Climate and environment; if we are in a stressed, polluted or dangerous environment, we will obviously benefit from the change, similarly there are some climates that are better than others, if you have a breathing problem, the principle applies.

Mental suggestion; the Bible says 'as a man thinketh in his heart, so is he', we can talk ourselves into emotional pain, and even physical sickness, or we can enjoy freedom and health (Prov 23.7, 15.15) a positive and trusting attitude frees the resources our body needs to stay healthy.

Deliverance from fears, guilts, bitterness; 'Ammon was so upset by his passion ... that it made him ill' (2 Sam 13.2 Moffatt, see also Psalm 31.9-10, Prov 14.30, 17.22). A mind at ease is life and health, but passion makes man rot away. Can you think of a time when someone was 'eaten up' with worry or anger or stress? There also occasions when a person needs to be delivered from demonic influences too (Luke 13.10-13).

Direct action by the Holy Spirit; it is often only the miracles and gifts of healings that Christians will give God credit for, fortunately God is not limited by that, there are many examples of miraculous healing (Acts 5.14-16 etc.).

Resurrection; Jones writes, 'Some diseases must await the final cure of the resurrection ... some of the saints of the earth have not been healed – they have lain on beds of unrelieved suffering. Then does God not will to heal? Yes, but He postpones it for some, to await the fullest cure in the resurrection.' The promises and purposes of God for us, and His provision do not end for us at death; it only seems that way to us if we ignore HIS time-frame, when we see someone die we feel that promises are unfinished, but God sees them as nearly completed, awaiting only the resurrection from the dead.

Hands on

Take some time to answer these fully, as your answers will greatly enhance the value of the next chapter.

- What's most important to you in your personal relationships? (e.g. honesty, trust, passion, respect, etc.)
- What's most important to you in your relationship with God?
- What's most important to you in your family?
- What's most important to you in your church?
- What's most important to you in helping others?

Chapter 5

The Presuppositions NLP brings to Christian Changework

Introducing presuppositions. Every approach to understanding, helping and changing people comes with its own set of assumptions and presuppositions, which act as filtering mechanisms, letting us notice some information and not others. Atheists assume there is no God therefore they WILL not 'see' the obvious hand of the Creator in their lives! Christians likewise have a set of presuppositions, many of the values in previous chapters are among them. The two main questions we must ask are 1) is this consistent with Biblical truth and values? and 2) is it effective? To get better results in what we do we must often adopt better more empowering beliefs, whether praying, witnessing or driving a car. When we are trained in caring or counselling we often take on our teachers' presuppositions without knowing it by 'osmosis' – the things they say make perfect sense when viewed from their perspective, but we do need to have a chance to evaluate them critically, 1 Thess 5.21 says, 'Test everything, hold fast to what is good.' This is particularly important if we are going to 'spoil the Egyptians' and take treasures, we need to ensure that we are not led off in the wrong direction.

Hall and Bodenhamer offer the following questions to use on all 'hidden presuppositions', including those which we look at later:

- Does this fit with scripture?
- To what extent does it fit?

- In what way does it fit?
- In what way does it not fit?
- How could somebody effectively use this to improve their walk with God?
- How could somebody misuse this and do themselves and others damage?

Back in the 1970s Richard Bandler and John Grinder studied some of the most effective communicators and therapists around and 'modelled' them, i.e. found out not only specifically what they did and said and thought but 'went behind' that and discovered the beliefs and presuppositions they operated from that enabled them to get superior results. They set about finding 'the difference that makes the difference' between ineffective therapists and these 'wizards'. Rather than mismatching and looking for what wouldn't work or where people were broken and deficient they 'modelled human excellence' – the best of the best and then explicitly taught these essential skills, patterns and beliefs which they called 'models'. Bandler, being from a computer science background, noticed which patterns (or 'programmes') of thought, language and behaviour (the effects of linguistics and neurology) which consistently produced results The collection of models (and the attitude of curiosity which generated them) became known as neuro-linguistic programming or NLP for short. We are able to use them without having to subscribe to the materialistic worldview of the originators; similarly we may avoid the 'besetting sin' of all effective approaches – especially for some NLP practitioners – namely boastfulness. Here are some of the major presuppositions, (with some Biblical thoughts about them, to get you started) as you read them ask yourself 'how would I relate differently to others if I acted as if these are true?'

- *The map is not the territory*. The 'real world out there' is taken in by our five senses, what we see, hear, feel, smell and taste on the outside (with their accompanying limitations) and then 're-presented' in our minds using those same five senses (in our 'minds-eye, self-talk', etc.). This information is not reality (the territory) but is a *map* of it, when we consider that we filter this input through our beliefs (of what is possible) our values (of what's important and worth noticing) and then labelling process whereby we attach words to designate meaning and aid recall, we realise that we seldom (if ever) respond directly to reality, but rather our incomplete perception of it. Another way of stating this is 'the menu is not the meal'. The Jews were responding to their maps in not being able to 'see' Jesus for who He was (John 1.11) As Christians we know that we are also spiritual beings and that until we are born again our spiritual eyes and senses are 'dull', blind and dead, so there is a lot of information that is missing from our maps until we receive 'revelation knowledge' to update our 'sense knowledge' maps. With God as Creator we can rephrase a verse to say 'Before the territory was, I AM', God is the ground of our being and of truth, our goal is to make our maps consistent with the Biblical map which is the accurate representation of reality and God. It is helpfully humbling to know that our map is not the territory, we do not have the monopoly on truth, and we can change our lives for the better as we update our maps.

— *Experience has a structure*. It is not only WHAT we think about (for example a memory of your mother or a friend), but HOW we think about it (is the image of them a black and white snapshot over there in the distance? Or are they close, moving, in colour and can you hear their voice? Swap over these characteristics and notice the change in feelings, then swap them back again.) Therefore to change something you don't necessarily need the content, just a small change in the *structure* can profoundly affect your subjective experience of the memory (how would you feel if that negative, criticising internal voice had a friendly, or seductive, tone of voice?). Movie directors use this, changing the camera angle from observing a car chase to having a driver's eye view will engage our feelings – we may even swerve on the sofa or put our feet down hard on the brakes!

— *The mind and body are parts of the same system*. This means they operate on a 'cybernetic loop', meaning simply the condition and use of our physiology affects how we represent things internally (if you are tired, run down or in pain, you 'see' the world differently to when you are full of beans) and of course, what and how we represent in our minds affects our physiology (resting on the sofa, watching a thriller on TV, you can find your heart is pounding and your muscles are tense!) For powerful examples of the effect of emotions on the body see Psalm 22.14-15. It is also this factor that makes placebos so effective, a person's belief in the pill is what changes the body, not the inert ingredients – there is a whole field of research that is developing ways of safely using the mind-body link in fighting illness and aiding recovery called Psycho-neuro-immunology. Do you think that attitudes like love, peace, contentment, harmony, faith, joy and hope would produce different results in your body than anger, bitterness, resentment, jealousy and depression?

– *Underlying every behaviour is a positive intention*, even if it is not positive for others, and because it hails from the past is now inappropriate, the original behaviour had a positive intention for the individual, usually to meet one of the basic human needs. This would mean that we can hold the positive worth of the individual but be free to question and challenge the appropriateness of internal and external behaviour. One of the keys to Jesus' ministry was that He came not to judge but to save (John 3.17), He knew that a person is more than their behaviour. From a Christian viewpoint we could add that sin is destructive and any demonic influence will have no positive intention at all. By assuming some positive intention we provide space for the person to change because we separate the person from the behaviour, and the behaviour from the intention, we then have a new direction to move in to find Biblical behaviour that meets legitimate needs. This leads to a corollary which is that

– *People always make the best choices (they perceive as) available to them,* which is why in the change-work we do, a major outcome is increasing the clients choice. We seldom would choose to do stupid, painful and destructive things if we were aware of pleasant, intelligent or fruitful alternatives we were aware of – the prodigal son didn't set out to be evil or depraved, he wanted adventure and made the best choices he *thought* were available (you also have been 'stuck' in a mental rut, unable to see alternatives, when with hindsight you realise you could have done something else, have you not?). The ultimate example of this attitude is Jesus' cry, 'Father forgive them for they know not what they do' (Luke 23.34). Sometimes we engage in 'maladaptive' behaviour because we just don't know of a healthy alternative or how to access that alternative – other times of course our motives are distorted by temptation. This is why Christian transformation has so much to do with renewing our minds, our maps become more accurate and we find that we have choice where we felt we had no choice before (see 1 Cor 10.13 there is always an escape).

- *If what you are doing isn't working, do something else – anything else!* This effectively reframes failure as 'feedback' which is designed to help the person keep adjusting in accomplishing their goals. The flexibility and tenacity that we need to have as Christians is embodied in this; for us though the 'anything else' does not include sinful behaviour. Tony Robbins once defined insanity as taking the same actions over and over again and expecting different results! We see a fly banging its head on the same pane of glass, when the open window is only inches away, it just needed to do something else! How many Christians do you know that do ineffective and labour intensive 'ministry' and won't give it up because they want to be 'faithful'? May God bless their faithfulness, and lead them into something else. The church growth movement talked about this when they said 'go to receptive groups, if a group is resistant hold them lightly, pray for them and get stuck into the receptive harvest until the "resistant" group are ripe.' There is too much left of the Great Commission to get side-tracked into things that don't work, the same applies to our individual lives.

- *The meaning of a communication is the response you elicit:* this is an application of the feedback / failure presupposition. For example, if you intend to say something caring and supportive to a friend, but they respond angrily, rather than blaming them and thinking how stupid they are to have misunderstood, you take it as feedback that you didn't communicate your intention in a way that worked (learn something), so you keep responsibility and 'try something else' *until* you have made yourself understood (this does not include the 'Englishman abroad' approach of repeating yourself LOUDER and s-l-o-w-e-r!), we can be gentle, gracious, truthful and flexible. While this holds true and is useful in human relationships, the meaning of the Bible is what is says, and sometimes we will get that wrong, also for example the law is good and holy but the response it elicits is to provoke sin! (Rom 6 and 7) In human communication we can say 'resistance is a comment about the inflexibility of the communicator', which should inspire us to be more tenacious, passionate, clear *and* flexible in what we are aiming for and how we are going about it. In God's communication we can only marvel at His clarity and creativity in using the Bible, the Church, circumstances, conscience and even our pain (C.S. Lewis said 'God whispers to us in our pleasures, speaks to us in our consciences and shouts at us in our pain') but pre-eminently in His Son (Heb 1.3) the word made flesh (John 1.12-14).

– *Individuals have two levels of communication, conscious and unconscious* We will discuss shortly what we mean by these terms, but isn't it true that on top of the words we say, there is all our 'body language'? The voice tone, gestures and postures will either confirm or contradict our message, you may have seen a person saying 'yes' with their mouth while shaking their head 'no', we cannot not communicate and often the unconscious communication is more simple and honest than the words we are offered.

– *I believe in unconscious learning* – my school teachers would agree with that! Let's back up a little and decide what we mean by these terms … imagine you went into a library late at night with a flash light, what you point that small circle of light at can symbolise your conscious mind, everything else in your library, every word, picture and book that you are not focusing on symbolises your unconscious. Some people like a computer analogy, your conscious mind is like the monitor, your unconscious mind is all the hardware in the box and operating system that allows input from the keyboard or stored images from your hard drive to be displayed in consciousness. Research shows that the conscious mind can attend to around seven bits of information at a time, less if we are under stress (Miller). Our nervous system may be receiving up to two million bits of information per second, this information is almost entirely outside of your conscious awareness (aren't you glad you don't have to remember to make your heart beat?) add to this that everything you've ever seen, heard, felt, smelled, tasted, read, imagined and said to yourself is recorded in some way in your unconscious mind. This is also where our habitual patterns are stored, and this is of great interest to us. You see there are four stages of learning: let's use driving a car as an example:

stage 1)   unconscious incompetence; simply stated: 'I don't know that I can't drive'

stage 2)   conscious incompetence; I've had my first lesson and now I know I can't drive!

stage 3)   stage conscious competence; I can now drive, but I have to think about my feet, the pedals, the gears, the speedo AND other drivers!

stage 4)   stage unconscious competence; at last all those actions have 'dropped' into my unconscious, I just do them automatically and can now listen to the radio, talk and drive safely.

Sounds great doesn't it, and it is part of the glorious way God made us. Unfortunately sometimes we have learned things wrong, or have habits that we can't uproot, but if you ask a good driver how he does it he can't tell you, 'it just happens'. Ask someone with a debilitating habit and they will say the same. To relearn safe driving we have to cycle back to stages 2 and 3 repeatedly until we get it right and then we can allow it to automate again, and we will then get the results we want, effortlessly and automatically – the good news is we can do this with our thoughts, and our behaviours. The other thing I mean by unconscious learning is that if you imagine that your conscious mind is a cup, and it is held over a well (your unconscious), if we are wanting to change some of the things you are drawing up from your well (say we want to purify it), we can either do that by getting new cupfuls and dealing with each one individually (the traditional approach to therapy and counselling) or we can pour something new and potent into the cup and let it overflow into the well (i.e. doing some things in conscious and unconscious mind simultaneously) or bypass the cup and chuck our cleaner into the well (some traditional forms of directive hypnosis). I personally favour the middle approach as it seeks to give choice and respects the integrity of the individuals.

In summary let's think once more about 'Failure vs. feedback', imagine Jesus operating from a 'failure frame' in Mark 6.1-6 'I tried, but they just wouldn't listen, it's not my fault, I mean – what could I do?' did He quit when faced with doubt and unbelief, did He blame and call them stupid? Of course not, He was flexible and changed His approach 'He went in a circuit around the villages teaching' this wasn't escaping a 'bad gig' but addressing the need – 'faith comes by hearing the word' Rom 10.17. So let's remember, all results are achievements, whether they are the desired results for a given task or not and therefore we cannot fail if we have an attitude open to learning and changing (Heb 5.14).

Hands on

- Try on' each presupposition, think through things that have gone well for you, would they fit? What would have happened if you had acted 'as if' they were true? How about when things went wrong, would you have had more choices if you acted 'as if' they were true? Would they help?

Part Two

The practical skills you've been waiting for

Chapter 6

Learning to be a detective

In this section of the book we are going to move on from having laid a theoretical foundation and start to build skills, approaches and techniques. Be warned, you are going to have things to do! The disciples rapidly realised that it wasn't enough just to follow Jesus and be where he was, they had to *pay attention*, they had to *get active in your learning*. In this chapter you will learn and experience some of the psychological models that neurolinguistics draws from, and then aquire some of the basic approaches to using them. The later chapters in part 2 will give detailed skill-sets for you to begin to use. Just as a detective, through his training, learns to look for what the rest of us miss, allow yourself to pick up insights for learning to model Jesus and to help others change. A warning first: I will be using neurolinguistic skills and patterns to teach you, using recurring trains of thought, stories and ungrammatical sentences – at times parts may appear confusing or illogical – this is completely intentional, and is a sign that you are doing well.

Learning, linking.

Generally speaking we are not aware how we have learned the things we have learned and incorporated into our repertoire of behaviours, or why for that matter, so we need to loop round and focus in on how we learn and how we do what we do, so we can use the relearning part of the four stages of learning.

Initially we learn by direct experience. If as an infant you put your hand over a flame your body would feel the pain and respond by moving it. Humans are great at one-time learnings, especially if they involve intense feelings (a phobia is an example of one trial learning, you don't have to try to remember to freak out when you see a spider!) but sometimes we link up the wrong stimuli with the feeling, so we may put our hand over the flame again and this time maybe we *associate* the feeling with the flame, we link them together in our minds. A caring parent will then teach us a word like 'Hot, ouch' and through repetition link that with the image of the flame and the feelings of burning pain. Later in life we find a thing called 'boiling kettle', this does not look like a flame but Mum says 'Hot, ouch' and so we learn by associating the word (which now represents the feeling) to the kettle and we avoid the pain of touching it. Each experience we have either goes into a 'pigeon hole' or creates a new one, and as we learn *language* we label the boxes which we put subsequent experiences into. We have a vast reference library of events, images, sounds and feelings and depending on the languaging and meanings we give them, we will have a rich resource of wisdom, or a limiting and painful one. Many schools then build on this reference library with a *'this is like that'* approach, if I wanted to tell you about how an electrical dimmer switch worked and you had not encountered electricity before I may say that it is like a water tap that increases or decreases the 'flow' to the light bulb – I take something that you do know, and link something to it by association – 'this is like that'. Jesus was a master at this, read Matthew 13, 'The Kingdom of God is like …', John's language in Revelation is the same 'He who sat on the throne was like jasper, etc.'. The quality of our lives is affected by the quality of references and the clarity of our filing (languaging) system, if I asked you to think of a dog, you go on a 'Transderivational search' (TDS) for the meaning of the word, you open the file, and access images of dogs you have known, any intense memories you may have – pleasant holidays walking the hills with your collie or unpleasant feelings of being barked at or even bitten. Using a general word like dog, your mind has to go on an extensive search inside a large box (assuming you have experiences of dogs) to 'make sense' of it, if I had asked you to think of a small brown dog, that specificity helps you to know what I am trying to communicate. If you think about it now, have you ever been in a conversation and assumed that you knew what each other meant? I remember getting terribly confused once when talking with a colleague about 'Dr M. Erickson' – he meant Milton Erickson a medical doctor and therapist, I meant Millard Erickson the theologian, I kept thinking 'I'm sure he wouldn't have said *that*!' A similar thing can happen when believers talk with Mormons, they use the same words but have different meanings.

In the brain the process of linking up what is new to what is known actually forms connections (Minirith) it's as if a thought were a path across a farmer's field, the more it is used, the wider it becomes (or the stronger the connection) if a thought or experience is intensely emotional in terms of pleasure or pain, it is like driving a lawnmower along the path. Through repetition or emotional intensity some of these neural pathways or *'neuro-associations'* can become six lane motorways! These tend to be the habitual and consistent thoughts, feelings and actions that shape our lives. Peak performance coach Anthony Robbins says, 'There are two reasons for human behaviour: 1) the need to avoid pain, and 2) the desire to gain pleasure. In order to efficiently evaluate how to rapidly accomplish these two tasks, the brain creates neuro-associations (associations within the nervous system) to instantly determine the meaning (pain / pleasure) of situations, people, things, sounds, emotions, etc. These neuro-associations are the driving force of most habitual behaviour. Our direction in life is based upon the neuro-associations of pain and pleasure linked in our nervous systems to certain situations, people, ideas, emotions or contexts. By changing these neuro-associations, we change the way we evaluate, the way we feel and, therefore, the way we behave.'

Pleasure and pain, motivation by carrot and stick.

At the most basic these levels are what drive our behaviour, they are part of God's design in our neurology – they keep us alive, protect us and motivate us. When we look in the Bible we can see how God wants them to work for us, they give us a direction to move away from (pain) and a direction to move towards (pleasure) they create in us a 'propulsion system' a push and pull that moves us in the right direction. In Deuteronomy 28 we read the blessings (pleasure) to move towards by obedience and faithfulness, and cursings (pain) to avoid, this is a perfect example of an aligned motivation, there are no conflicting elements. In Hebrews we have the warnings of wrath and the promises of glory; in Jesus' teaching we have the ultimate pain of Hell graphically presented, as well as the pleasure of heaven, e.g. Luke 16 Lazarus and the rich man.

Understanding this two-pronged form of motivation means we can help ourselves and our clients. Interestingly it's not what happens to us that sets our direction, but the meaning we give to what happens to us, for most of us being flogged in public would mean major pain, the apostles however gave it a different meaning 'they departed ... rejoicing that they were counted worthy to suffer shame for His name' (Acts 5.41), much of what you will learn in this book will enable you to change meanings to live more fully as a follower of Christ. Outside of scripture meanings are not fixed, so we can choose those which empower us in Christian living. It is worth stating here that generally we will do more to avoid pain than to gain pleasure – it is a gut level survival instinct given us by God – this is why many fears can be so debilitating, they are moving away from something that probably is not real. Colin Urqhuart uses the letters in fear to stand for 'False Expectations Appearing Real'. My experience of pastoral caring and counselling has shown me that many well-meaning folk have either linked pain or pleasure to the wrong things, and now feel 'trapped' in behaviours they know are wrong but are powerless to change because they are motivated at the neuro-associative (gut) level, let's see how this happens ...

'Anchors away'.

Does the name Pavlov ring a bell? He was the scientist who developed the concept of classical conditioning. His most famous experiments were those where he took hungry dogs, and as he offered them food rang a bell, he did this consistently whenever the dogs were in a peak state of hunger and salivation, later he rang the bell and the dogs salivated – the bell had become associated to the state of hunger. In modern times this *stimulus / response* mechanism has been called 'anchoring'. Humans are stimulus/response creatures too, although because of our ability to create and change meaning and language we are (or at least should be) far more than that. Anchors can occur in any of our senses, visual anchors that access and revive emotional states are old photos, the Cross, Americans respond strongly to the Stars and stripes flag. There is a Royal Mail ad that runs: 'I saw this ... and thought of you' – this is the power of association. Think about this, have you ever had the experience of responding irrationally to someone, or feeling bad in response to someone, and later found that it was because they 'gave you the look' that an angry parent or teacher gave you as a child? That is an example of how old anchors can get in the way of our present experience. Sometimes the anchor can be outside of our conscious awareness, but still evoke the feeling, my favourite example is 'our song' – remember when you fell in love, you felt intense emotions, if simultaneous to those feelings there was a song or piece of music consistently on the radio it could become an anchor for those feelings, it may even be 'your special song' – what would happen if you heard it again? Some of those feelings come back, because they are stored associated to the sounds are they not? Other sound anchors are voice tones, or imagine someone standing in the front of your class room and dragging their fingernails down the blackboard – I have asked various groups to do this and you can watch them cringe and wince, and it's not even happening! Closer to church, do certain hymns or worship songs that were significant to you in the past trigger those old memories and feelings in you still?

At this level many good worship leaders 'stack' (intensify) and reinforce positive feelings of worship, the presence of God, commitment and holiness and 'attach' them to certain songs; many liturgical churches do the same with the Lords Prayer or certain Psalms and rituals. This is not necessarily mechanistic or manipulative, but rather observing how things become more meaningful and learning from it. Feeling anchors can be various kinds of touch (person only has to grip my right shoulder in a certain way and I can 'hear' the voice of my old headmaster telling me off!), temperature ('On a hot day like today, I remember the summer of '76') also textures like silk or fur. Other anchors can be tastes or smells, have you never walked past a bread shop and remembered ...? Of course words are anchors that will evoke feelings and responses, how about the words 'dentist' or 'ecstasy'? Used skilfully words can evoke states and then link them to other stimuli. How about Jesus evoking a 'no worries' state and linking it to seeing birds and flowers? So does this mean that we are at the mercy of our environment, that our 'buttons' can just get pushed and we will feel all kinds of things in response? Yes, unless we decide to take responsibility and godly dominion over the process. We used to walk through life like emotional flypaper picking up whatever associations were offered us, often linking things up wrong or overgeneralising but now we know how it works we can set it up so it works for us. Do you think it would be useful to 'rewire' an anchor that used to send you into unresourceful states or sinful behaviour so that the SAME trigger now sent you in a totally new direction? There are *four keys to setting an effective anchor (do this on yourself first, choosing a positive emotion, and learn how to do this with others in the skills section)*

a) you need to access a fully associated state, what I mean by that is you are feeling the state fully in your body,

b) at the peak of that state you provide a simultaneous stimuli that will be associated to the feelings,

c) the stimulus or trigger is to be unique and consistent, let's have an example... If you wanted to anchor humour, you would first find a time when you were laughing, and while you were laughing, reach over and pull your earlobe (a touch anchor) pull a weird face (a visual anchor) and/or make an outrageous sound (auditory anchor) if you repeat this a couple of times, then change conversation (break the state – shake your body out, do something different) then you can ...

d) test the anchor by 'firing' off one of the those triggers and see if it elicits that response, if it does, your job is done.

Now, imagine I was anchoring humour with you and I had got you laughing and then shook your hand, is that a good anchor? Not really for two reasons, first it is not very unique so it will get mixed with other associations, and second, if the anchor did take, I don't know how appropriate bursting into laughter as you shake hands with your new boss might be! In the skills section of the book you will discover some powerful techniques using this simple tool. But just imagine, if you could gather up the powerful and godly resources you sometimes feel and anchored them so you could feel those more often, and when you need them most, that would change things, wouldn't it? And if you could neutralise the power of those environmental anchors that 'ring your bell' and get you behaving in ways you don't want to any more, you would really be moving in the right direction, you would have taken control of a gift God has given you, your neurology. We have been learning how we learn, how we link things up and how these can affect our emotional state, let's take this a step further and discover how we can change our state for even greater effectiveness and joy.

Behaviour model,

By now you know that all behaviour is meaningful, we always do things for a reason – to avoid the pain of an unmet need or maybe gain a higher level pleasure, but there is a little more to the equation than that ... our emotional state drives and modifies behaviour. Have you ever had a loved one or good friend be harsh and unjust to you? Often when that happens we lose sight of who they really are and what they really mean to us, I mean, they are not normally like that, that's not why we love them or choose to have them as our friends, so what's going on?

There is more to each of us than what we do, sometimes we do and say things that are quite out of character, but we often excuse ourselves by saying something like 'I wasn't feeling myself' or 'I was in a terrible state' these descriptions are very accurate.

As human beings we have tremendous potential to produce behaviours that support us and those around us in living healthy and happy lives, but often our behaviour does not reflect our potential, that is because *our state determines or at least affects our behaviour.* What I mean by state is the present mood, focus and condition of your mind and body, for example, have you found that you produce different behaviours when you are in a state of rage to a state of loving gentleness? How about a happy vibrant state compared to tired and depressed? I say again *our behaviour is affected by and is a result of our state.* There are two basic kinds of state – those that empower us to live happy and useful Christian lives and those that are disempowering, and cause us to be ineffective, unhappy and even compromise or dishonour our relationship with Christ

Now, do you think it may be useful to be able to access powerful and resourceful states when you need them? Or to be able to change your state from fearful and powerless to confident trust and action? Would your involvement in the Great Commission be altered if you could step out of doubt and procrastination into faith and boldness?

We are able to control our state and therefore alter the results that we produce, and as we see and experience what we are getting this in turn affects our beliefs about what is possible, what could be normal and also just how good, exciting and fruitful being a disciple can really be, and more importantly, that the Bible is full of examples and illustrations of just this happening.

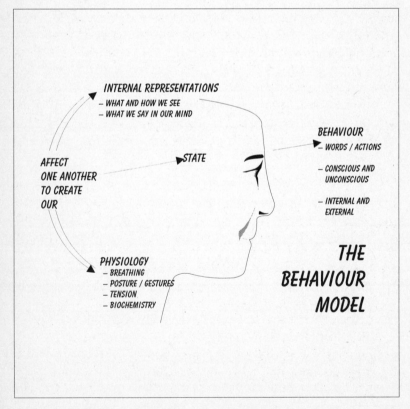

INTERNAL REPRESENTATIONS
– WHAT AND HOW WE SEE
– WHAT WE SAY IN OUR MIND

BEHAVIOUR
– WORDS / ACTIONS

– CONSCIOUS AND UNCONSCIOUS

– INTERNAL AND EXTERNAL

AFFECT ONE ANOTHER TO CREATE OUR

STATE

PHYSIOLOGY
– BREATHING
– POSTURE / GESTURES
– TENSION
– BIOCHEMISTRY

THE BEHAVIOUR MODEL

To illustrate how our mental-emotional state is created by a 'configuration' of mind and body, just imagine that outside your door was a man with 'depression', picture in your mind what he would look like, would he be standing tall, head up, chest out, breathing deeply and regularly, a smile on his face? Chances are that his head would be down, shoulders slumped, eyes down, breathing shallow, facial muscles flaccid. One side of what creates our emotional state is our *physiology,* but there is more, our state is also directly affected by what happens inside our brain too, the things we say to ourselves, and the things that we picture, we will refer to these as our *internal representations* (i.e. what we represent to ourselves on the inside). Also the things that we believe have a tremendous impact on what we experience.

Physiology and internal representations work in what is called a 'cybernetic loop' (cyber is the word for 'steersman', a person who adjusts what he is doing in an ongoing way in response to feedback – where he's going and where he's pointing at the moment) this means that our physiology affects our internal representations, (for example, when you are feeling ill, in pain or very tired, don't you sometimes perceive things differently to when you are feeling fresh, alert and in good health?) and also that our internal representations affect our physiology, for example, if you vividly remember anything frightening, your heart will start racing, and you experience an increase in muscle tension.

Try this exercise:

1) remember a time when you felt particularly good, a specific pleasant memory, what did you see at the time? Remember it as if you are seeing it again through your own eyes, what did you feel at the time? Hear those things again, how did that feel? Can you remember that feeling fully, now?

2) think of a time in the past, when just through worrying or rerunning painful memories caused you to get into a disempowering state – don't relive it, just recall that choice back then and put the past behind you.

3) remember a time when you understood something clearly, if you can't think of a time, just act as if you did, and move your body – how would you be standing or sitting if you

really got a grip on something new? What would your face look like? How would you be breathing? what would you say to yourself when you knew you really had it? Adjust your body that way and feeling that way now, simply remember that you body can lead your mind, and your mind can lead your body, to produce new states that create the Christian behaviour that you want.

If you went to church with a camcorder and walked around, what would you see? You could almost certainly find people worshipping and praying, if this is all you focused on you would come away thinking 'what a spiritual church', you may also be able to find people complaining or moaning, if you focused on them you would feel a whole lot different wouldn't you? At the same church you could find and *focus* on people who were doing too much, and others not doing anything at all, and each time your feelings would flow from what you chose to focus on, and by default what you chose to delete from attention. That is the content side of our internal representations, but how about the *structural attributes* – if you saw someone arguing, or even criticising you for having the camcorder at church how would it feel as you 'zoomed out' and made them more distant, especially if you turned the sound down? Or 'zooming in' right close to their angry mouth and having bad words in stereo! There are many structural changes that have a massive impact on our state, for example how close an image is, how big, how bright, or whether sounds are distant and 'tinny' or close and full and loud. Some of the more pervasive we could even think of as *Internal Filters* for the camcorder, these would dramatically change not only *what* you would see but *how* you would see, these would include your values and beliefs, memories, decisions, language, attitudes and some filtering devices called meta-programmes (see later).

Can you now see why people can have so many reactions to the same event? It is true that we seldom respond directly to the environment, or that 'perception is projection' – this is actually good news because it means that most people are able to overcome their problems by adopting a new perspective – you are learning the tools that will help them with how.

The Bible calls us to 'set our minds on things above' (Col 3.1) and on 'whatever is pure, lovely, good, etc. (Phil 4.8).

As well as the focus of our mind in terms of what and how we focus, there is also our words that affect our state, firstly our *'self-talk'* – if we talked to others the way we sometimes talked to ourselves, we'd get arrested! What are some of the things you say to yourself? Do you constantly criticise, question your ability to do things or just plain insult yourself, or have you learned to build yourself up, speak nice to yourself, encourage and appreciate? Then there is the tone of voice we use with ourselves, harsh, attacking tonality does not motivate, it disempowers – how would you feel if that critical voice (which does have a good intention) was more polite? Or if it couldn't manage that how about if it sounded like John Wayne or Marilyn Monroe or a Smurf? Where is it coming from? is it right in your face? Behind you? What would it feel like to hear it coming from your elbow or your big toe? Would you be able to hear its message better without feeling bad? What about the *intensity of language,* some people are 'livid, furious and outraged' others language is softened and they are 'a little peeved, a tad put out!' but about the same happening! What about *questions*? do you think questions can direct the focus of your thinking? Do you remember the colour of your newest pair of shoes, did they take long to break in until they were comfortable? Do you see how questions direct your focus now? Listen out for questions that presuppose things, 'why can't I ever' presupposes you can't, 'why am I so stupid?' Doesn't set you up for an answer you want to hear! Finally we often speak and think in *metaphors*, life is a battle, I'm at the end of the road, I'm up the creek without a paddle, or life is a party, or a dance. Think about what it implies, if life is a battle there will be losers, casualties, if it is a dance, we move together, gracefully and all feel good. You will develop your appreciation and ability of these elements in the skills section later.

Just for fun, do this exercise with a friend and notice the effects: 'I want you close your eyes and take a deep breath, relax in your seat and take another deep breath and this time I want you to imagine you have nostrils in the soles of your feet and are sucking in oxygen up to your waist, great, now I want you to make a picture in your mind of a sunny beach, if you hate the beach then go to a nice fresh meadow, see the blue sky, hear the soft breeze in your ears and feel the softness under your feet, now describe your state ... next I want you to go to that beach but it is grey and raining, it must be Skegness! There is a flash of lightening and a distant roll of thunder, describe your state ... finally I want you to make a picture of the sunny beach, can you see it? And now hear the thunder, what does that do? Did you feel shifts in your body as a result of what was happening in your head? Isn't it incredible that all of us are affected by our internal representations?'

Mind-Body, Body-Mind: Physiology

The other end of the mind-body loop is that our *physiology* affects our state and therefore our internal representations. First is the issue of the *condition* of our body. If we are tired, or in pain, if we think we are going down with the flu it affects the way we feel and think. Often we don't notice when we feel good, just when we do not. A major part of physiology is our *biochemistry*, think about it, why do people smoke, drink alcohol, comfort eat or take drugs? Because they change our biochemistry and therefore the way we feel they distract our body into pleasurable feelings just like shopping or TV distracts our focus. Fortunately there are many healthy alternatives, exercise, sport, and just the good feeling of healthful vitality. Lastly, the way we move radically affects our state, remember our depressive? Try this: stand up, throw your shoulders back, breath deeply, look up, put a big smile on your face and now feel depressed without changing your physiology at all – I know you can't do it. The speed of our *movement* also, try skipping down the road, or explosively conducting to Beethoven, it changes your state AND anyone else who sees you! Think now about worship in the Psalms, lifting up your eyes, bowing, clapping, shouting with a voice of triumph, God has given us good emotions that are strong and that we can direct in our praise and service of Him.

Here's a fun exercise called the 'capewalk': 'walk round the room slowly, looking down at the ground, shoulders slumped, shallow breathing, now stop, shake your body out, and I want you to stride round the room, head up, breathing deep and strong, but this time I want you to walk as if you had a silk Batman cape on, or you're a vampire (only pretend, don't bite each other!) and you have this long flowing cape – Yeah, that's it – OK who noticed a difference? Did anyone not notice a difference? Can you check his pulse? Oh you did, what was it? Confident? How come just walking made you confident; it couldn't be that simple could it? Can you see how just becoming aware of these things could have a major impact on how you spend the day tomorrow; and you don't even have to have the cape dry cleaned!'

Another major component to add into the 'mind' end of the mind-body connection is *beliefs.*

Beliefs are the controlling force in perception and action an old cliché says, 'If you believe you can, or you believe you can't – you're right.' Our beliefs operate as attractors in our thinking, they will notice what reinforces them, and will disregard what contradicts them. Psychology calls this 'cognitive dissonance'. Have you ever tried to compliment a person with low self-esteem? They just shrug it off, they 'know' you don't mean it and are only saying it, because it doesn't fit with their existing beliefs. My favourite illustration for explaining beliefs is if you imagine that an idea is a tabletop, it needs legs to support it, those legs are 'reference experiences', so for example if you have the idea 'I'm a kind person', can you think of any examples to back that up? The more legs, or the stronger the legs (i.e. emotionally charged references), the more you have a sense of certainty. 'Tables' come in three strengths, 1) opinions, being preferred ideas, 2) beliefs, which are usually unconscious and control much of our thinking and behaving, and 3) convictions, which are so solid and emotionally charged we may even feel angry or offended if they are challenged. Once we have accepted an idea, we then go on a search for references to back it up, we do the same with a theological belief too, do we not? Now, if I asked you if you could believe that life is full of pain and disappointment, could you think of examples from your own experience and the daily news? Of course. How about the belief that life is full of opportunities and joy? Yes, you could do that too – so which is right? Both are, but which will enable you to tap your resources and enjoy a better quality of life? The latter obviously. We can choose what we believe, what we feel certain of – but what if you already have limiting and disempowering beliefs, can you change them? The thing that keeps a table stable is that we don't question it, we assume it is correct, it therefore filters new information in the light of itself. The way to 'knock the legs from the table' is to start questioning it again, for *as soon as* we question it, we feel less sure. Here are some questions we could ask that would do this: is this always true? When is it not true? What's ridiculous about this? How could the opposite actually be true? Does this square with all of Biblical truth? What are the exceptions?

As we go through life our brain constantly asks 'will this mean pain or pleasure, and what am I going to do?' As we pick up the ideas of others and provide our own legs for them we develop beliefs as to was will cause pain or pleasure. To add in the logical levels, we then discover that we value moving towards some states of pleasure more than others, and seek to avoid some states of pain more than others, and then we have the (often unspoken) rules that operate and drive our behaviour that say 'if I do this, then I'll feel that', the exercises at the end of this chapter are some of the most powerful you can use with yourself and others, because when we become consciously aware of our values and rules, we can then change them if they do not support us in living the Christian life.

Cybernetics

God created us with a need to be purposeful, or to have goals – Adam and Eve's is found in Gen 1.28, as they looked and saw an unpopulated and unsubdued earth, they could see their goal, they had a 'present state', and a 'desired state', and needed resources and action to bridge the gap, of course they had to keep checking on how they were doing. Simply put the study of cybernetics is just that, cyber comes from the word 'steersman'. If you imagine an ocean liner travelling from England to America, the destination is programmed into the computer or mapped out in the captains mind, but wind, currents and other traffic will mean constant monitoring and readjustment to get there. I occasionally let my young children steer the car while I operate the pedals, they are always amazed that they need to keep adjusting and changing, they can't just point it in the right direction and leave it. A cybernetic system works on a unit called a TOTE, which stands for *Test, Operate, Test, Exit*, imagine your radio is too loud for you a TOTE would run like 'Test: it's too loud, Operate: turn it down, Test: is it right now? if no go back to Operate, if yes, go to Exit'. It is an ongoing feedback / adjustment programme much like those used in computers.

As a guitarist I am constantly running a TOTE of 'is my guitar in tune, if not is such and such a string sharp or flat, as I adjust it is it closer to being in tune or further away? and I exit only when I am satisfied – this brings me to the next important point, which concerns a part of your brain called the *reticular activation system (RAS).* Because there are potentially millions or billions of bits of information your nervous system could pay attention to, it has to screen out the vast majority, or we would be overloaded and go mad. We tell our RAS what is important, and therefore what to notice and the more specific we are the more effective it becomes, for example my 'ear' is more sensitive than that of a beginning guitarist, because I have made finer distinctions of pitch. An example of the RAS working would be, have you ever decided to buy a new car, and then noticed all the cars for sale in your area? Or if you were more specific, say you decided on a yellow VW Beetle, suddenly you 'see them everywhere', they were there before, you just hadn't told your RAS to notice them. How can this help us? try this experiment with a friend: ask them to look around the room, and notice everything that is brown, wood, clothing, furniture, books, all shades of brown – now shut your eyes and list everything green … it's not fair is it? Unless they were very familiar with their surroundings, they can't do it, but as they open their eyes again of course they will almost involuntarily notice the green. The relevance to our quality of life is this, Do you know people who focus on everything that is 'brown' in life? Have you noticed that they are so good at it that they screen out everything that is green (and growing)? We choose what we will notice, We choose what will reinforce our beliefs, our joy and our gratitude; or not.

Another thing the RAS is great for is marshalling our resources, when we tell it what we want to do, it notices everything that can help us in that direction – this is where **goal setting** can come in, and of course because the RAS operates within our 'cybernetic' brain it takes in ALL results, positive and negative and views them as feedback to help us get on or stay on course – there is no failure, only feedback! When we set goals or outcomes, the more precise we are, the clearer we programme our RAS, the more we will notice what is in the way, and what will help us. I remember hearing a 'three minute seminar' on setting outcomes which had four points:

- know what you want,

- take intelligent action,

- notice what results you are getting,

- keep changing your approach until you get what you want.

This is sound advice whether we want to prepare a talk, be a better husband or wife, be more Christlike, help fulfil the Great Commission or improve your performance at work or as a parent training your children. God has made us purposeful, and the Bible, and both Jesus and Paul show us the power of a goal oriented life (read John 4.34 and Phil 3.13-14). Neurolinguistics help us be more specific about how to do this, the *'outcome frame'* gives us eight steps to take our goals through:

1) Outcomes should be stated positively, the mind does not process negatives, if I say to you 'Don't think of an elephant' what happens? you have to 'make sense' of the words, so you have to represent the word 'elephant' in your head. Paul Had this trouble in Rom 7.15 'I do not understand what I do. For what I want to do I do not do, but what I hate I do.' I have had countless people come to me and tell me what they DON'T want – but guess what they get more of because of their focus? So the first thing is to state it positively, rather than 'I don't want to feel sad like this anymore' how about 'I want to feel great from now on'? Also focusing on what you DO want stops us slipping into blaming or excusing (see the exercise on the 'blame frame') as well as our propulsion system gone wrong – in our desire to move away from pain, we could 'jump out of the frying pan and into the fire' before you jump, ask yourself these

questions, 'what <u>do</u> I want? specifically? What will having that do for me? have I stated this positively?

2) Next they should be stated using sensory based language, your RAS needs an evidence procedure to know whether it has got what it is going for or needs to keep adjusting, by sensory based I mean you answer these questions, 'how will I know when I get it? What will I see? What will I hear? What will I feel? What will I say to myself? Are there any other ways that I would know?

3) Our outcomes need to be self initiated and controlled, if you put your outcomes at the mercy of others it not only disempowers you from taking action (because you are waiting for them to do it) and also sets you up for disappointment. Has anyone ever asked you 'how can I change my spouses (or boss, or children etc.) behaviour?' The real answer is 'Easy, change *your* behaviours and responses to them in some way that leaves them without the need or context for their old behaviour, now what do YOU need to do that?' Useful questions to ask are, 'do you and you alone control your outcome? Does it involve anyone else? Can you initiate and maintain the responses needed?

4) Our outcomes need to be appropriately contextualised. You probably know that not all behaviour is appropriate everywhere! so ask yourself, 'do I want my outcome all the time? In all places? With all people? Without limitations? Where / when would it be inappropriate? Where / when / how and with whom do I want this outcome? Have you noticed that your RAS is really 'getting the picture', but for us to really be able to confidently and fully reach for our goals we have four more steps to walk through;

5) Settle 'secondary gain'. If all behaviour gives us some positive value or benefit, then for change to be permanent and fulfilling, we must at least equal or redirect the secondary gain of pleasure our old state had, this is why so many people struggle with overeating or smoking, they do not account for what the old behaviour gave them, and find a healthy and enjoyable alternative, ask 'what has the old behaviour given me? What would I lose if I changed? When / where / with whom would my outcome not feel ok?

6) To get from our present state to our desired state we need *resources*, so a well formed outcome has the resources built into it so it is believable and practical, ask, 'what do I have

now, and what do I need to achieve this outcome? Have I ever done 'X' before? Do I know anyone else who has done 'X' before? can I 'chunk down' the resources into smaller blocks that may be more achievable / available?

7) One of the things that impressed me most about NLP was its emphasis on checking the ecology of a change or outcome, Hall says 'Ecology …, as the science of the relationship between an organism and its environment, speaks in NLP about our concern that changes made at one point in a human system must fit together with and adapt to the other parts of the system in a healthy way.' Classic examples from our culture is the man who works late to 'be a success' or 'provide for my family' whose health breaks down or is never there for his children – the outcome is noble, but accomplished unecologically, Areas of ecology check are family / work / school / friends / community / spirituality / health.

8) The last set of questions are those from Cartesian logic, which give us one last chance to view the outcome from different angles and feel if it still rings true, ask 'what will happen if I get it? What won't happen if I get it? What will happen if I don't get it? What won't happen if I don't get it?' I know these questions stretch your brain, but if your outcome comes through intact, then the last things to do are, go for it, notice what you're getting, keep adjusting till you get what you want!

Hands on

You will go through a complete goal-setting exercise in the skills section, so let's take some time to 'tie up' some more about you, thinking through the various levels of your personality – the kind of person you are is what dictates the kinds of things you can and will do, sit back and enjoy this process of self-discovery.

A: identity

grab a sheet of paper and answer these questions

1) if I were to look in a dictionary and find an entry under my name, what would it say? Would it list my talents? Achievements? What would it say about who I am?

2) what do you have in common with people and what makes you unique?

3) imagine writing a brief description of yourself for a passport, what roles, responsibilities, character attributes do you think are most important to list so the Customs officers will really know its you?

B: global beliefs

Finish the following sentences as many different ways as possible until you feel you have expressed your belief about them:

1) Life is … 2) People are … 3) Family is …
4) Work is … 5) God is … 6) My body is …
7) Money is … 8) I am …

C: values

Write down a list of the things that are important to you, make it as long as possible, then go over the list and ask yourself 'what's important to me about this?. Keep asking until you have turned all the 'things' into states, e.g. if you had 'work, car, money' you could ask yourself, what's important to me about these? Eventually you may get to answers like 'work gives me a sense of contribution, my car gives me a sense of freedom and status, and money gives me security'. This is the process of turning our 'means' values into 'ends' values – what we really want from the 'means'. When helping others, we can explore keys areas of values by asking 'what's important to you in ....' areas like spirituality, health, family, work, money, etc., when we have tracked down the 'end' value-states, we can help them improve their choices about which 'means' they will use as vehicles to achieve those 'ends'. (We will look in detail at ways to increase choice in our beliefs, values and rules in the chapter Christian Life Reframing)

D: rules

To find out our rules all we need to do is choose one of our values and ask 'how will I know when I've got it? Or what has to happen in order for me to feel it?' What we are looking for is an 'if / then' structure, for example if we are talking about my value of love, I may say, 'If you look at me and smile, then I know you love me', we can also do this in reverse when a person feels their rules have been violated – 'what has to happen for you to not feel loved?' 'If you don't smile at me, then I know you don't love me' (this is usually presented in an accusatory form 'I know you don't love me because you don't smile at me any more' or variations on the theme! more about how to identify and change these language patterns in the chapter on Precision). So, find out your rules, and those of the people who are closest to you, listen out for an 'if / then' or 'because' structure.

Practical Approaches to changework

Have you ever watched a good wine-taster or art critic? Have you ever gone to a doctor or specialist and had them 'read' your body like a book? The reason they can do this is they have developed sensory acuity, an acute sensitivity to particular bits of information that we don't notice. Have you ever spent time with someone new and 'bonded' almost immediately, there was that rapport and common understanding between you? Can you think of a time when you saw or heard someone who communicated powerfully, whose actions, gestures and voice tone backed up all that they said? These three attributes, sensory acuity, bonding power and congruency are all marks of a master communicator, think of Jesus, Paul or more recently Martin Luther King. Fortunately for us, through the modelling process we can now learn the skills that move us towards excellence too.

Sensory acuity

The story is told of a professor at a medical college for doctors who, in his opening lecture started to describe the sensory acuity needed to excel in medicine. 'For example,' he said, taking up a small glass pot, 'in here I have a urine sample from a man with pneumonia, just do what I do.' So saying he put a finger in the pot and raised his hand to his mouth, popping a finger in. The students reluctantly, but obediently copied, some coughed and gagged as they tasted the urine, after all the students had finished, the professor continued, 'It is better that you learn now from bitter experience, than with a patient the importance of paying attention – if you had been observant you would have seen me dip my index finger in the urine, and put my middle finger in my mouth!'.

Whenever we are talking with someone we must pay attention, because of the unconscious and non-verbal components of communication, there is a mine of information being given that we normally ignore. You cannot not communicate, whether it is the slight, involuntary head nod or a shaky and hesitant voice tone, we become aware sometimes of mixed messages, do we not? To be aware of our surroundings we have to be in 'uptime' with our senses focused on the external world. If you imagine your attention is a fingertip it can either be pointing out at something, or it can be curled inside a fist – it is still pointing at something, but focused inside, that is called 'downtime'. Have you ever been with someone and as you are talking they drift off? The lights are on but no-one's home! in the process of listening to each other, we occasionally have to go inside our heads to 'make sense' of the words they offer us, sometimes that TDS search can get distracted and we stay there – a word has evoked a memory or train of thought.

How about setting up an uptime anchor? Go through each sensory system one by one, start with visual and make sure you are totally 'visual external' and anchor it, repeat and reinforce, then go to auditory (hearing) external, same with smell, with kinesthetics, pay attention to temperature, pressure and weight, NOT emotions as they will draw you inside – anchor each of these in the same place (the same trigger), then fire it off so all senses are directed outside, an uptime anchor is useful in many situations, especially when helping others. Creating an anchor like this means that we have clean channels of communication, before we go on to list some of the things you can now begin to notice, a word of caution: Christians are bad mind readers! When we notice non-verbal communication, we must beware of hallucinating we know what it means. Some 'body language' books tell you that leaning back with arms and legs folded means you are 'closed.' It doesn't necessarily mean anything of the sort, it may just be comfortable. To make this point Richard Bandler tells of when he was visiting a group therapy and sat with legs crossed, the group leader told him that his body language meant he was 'closed to new ideas', Richard humorously replied that, 'that's not where new ideas go in, I think you've been doing it wrong!'. To avoid this mindreading and guesswork (which is a projection of *our maps* onto other peoples' behaviour) our descriptions need to be sensory based, in terms of see, hear, feel – if we then are able to find out what those mean to the person we can then link those descriptions to their corresponding emotional state, this is called *calibration*, and every person is different, and generalisations will often get us in trouble.

Hands On

Go through this list of statements and label S for sensory specific or M for mindreading (more about mindreading in the chapter on precision)

1. I knew his heart was going like the clappers
2. there was a sad expression on her face
3. her face went pale when her husband walked in.
4. she was relieved by the letter
5. his pupils dilated
6. she took a deep breath and blinked.
7. he looked anxious during the hearing
8. her palms were sweaty
9. you could see relief written all over his face
10 she flinched as he leaned toward her.

(answers at the end of the chapter)

sensory acuity – making finer distinctions, learning chunking skills:

Fire off your uptime anchor, begin to describe a real scene to yourself that you can see, either chunking down, e.g. 'I see two houses on a hill, I see four white windows on the left house, I see blue curtains in the top right window, I see floral design on the material, I see a pink rose on the curtain, I see a darker petal … etc.' Or chunking up. 'I see some waste paper in the street, I see the grass verge, I see the road and houses … etc.' Allow yourself to stretch to very small chunks.

 – Visual acuity: do this with a friend, get your friend to stand or sit in any position, take a mental snapshot and close your eyes, your friend starts by making major posture changes, and when you open your eyes you have to say what's different. As you get better, chunk down to very small shifts in movement.

- The 12 states of attention: for each of the three main modalities (visual, auditory and kinaesthetic) we can have internal or external focus, and also broad or narrow focus, this gives us a grid of states of attention. Noticing which states of attention we habitually use is the first step in mastering our thinking – if you are 'stuck' with a problem, 'try on' a different state of attention, you will probably find greater flexibility in your thinking and an enhanced ability to enjoy more. Most people in our culture have very low 'body awareness' and can only think of focus in terms of pain i.e. 'acute pain in my chest, or aches all over my body' – how about experimenting with pleasure instead?

- Outside / inside focus: next time you are in a conversation, or even better if you are watching a chat show, notice that at different intervals, a persons focus has to go inside, either to recall information or to process what has been said, this can be seen by such obvious things as averting of eyes, looking up or down, or even holding up the hands in a 'stop / slow down' gesture.

    This is useful for us to learn, because at the point that a person's focus is inside, it is not outside, and therefore they are more aware of their thoughts than what you are saying if you keep talking, in fact they may even feel pressured, hassled, or uncomfortable if you don't give them time to 'stay with you'.

    An important part of rapport is pacing this rate of input, or else much of what we say gets missed and also we put pressure on the other person.

    Can you think of a time when someone either deliberately or accidentally rode roughshod over you by not giving a chance to 'catch up' and how that diminished the effectiveness of their communication? Don't fall into the same trap, if you have something worth saying, make sure that they are listening to you.

- Minimal cues: take time to start to notice some of the smaller bits of body information available to you for example, a change in a person's breathing usually indicates a change in internal state, where are they breathing? High in the chest or low? What about tempo? Are the breaths fast, short and shallow? Slow and shallow? Deep and fast?

> Other minimal clues are the small muscle changes around the corners of the mouth, the jawline and the outer corners of the eyes. Look for tension or looseness. Also look for colour changes, in the neck, lower and upper cheek and forehead, there is much more to this than just blushing, notice how colour shifts on the cheeks as the person changes subjects in conversation. The flow of blood and muscle tension are seen clearly in the position and size of the lower lip, at this point simply notice these changes and see if you can calibrate them to any particular state or subject. The aim is to become 'sensory based' in our understanding, rather than project our feelings and meanings onto another.

Rapport

Have you ever wondered how come rapport happens with some people but not with others? Rapport is that sense of bonding or oneness or agreement or even just liking we get when we enter someone else's map of the world. We tend to like people who are like us, and when we are not like someone we may tend to 'have differences' with them. When God wanted to communicate with us, when He wanted to speak 'the last word' (Heb 1.3), He became like us, the incarnation is a perfect example of creating rapport – God became a man to speak to men (John 1.14, 18). When Paul wanted to preach the gospel, he did the same he would be 'to the Jews a Jew, to the Gentiles a gentile' (1 Cor 9.20), why? To remove unnecessary barriers to communication, if I go to Russia, I will not get far if I don't speak Russian – for me to take the initiative in building meaningful relationships I must learn to speak the other persons language. How about the same with non-verbal or 'body language'? would you be willing to do it for the sake of removing barriers and building meaningful relationships?

Matching and mirroring:

Some research indicates that out of our overall communication only 7% is in the words we speak, 38% is in how we speak, our voice tone, tempo and volume, and the remaining 55% is our physiology – but think about when you meet someone new, what do you pay most attention to? Is it your words? We often make conversation asking 'small talk' questions until we 'find something in common' and then start to relax with each other, how much is really based on the words, and how much on voice analogues or physiology? Michael Hall says 'gestures and voice tone speak volumes, while words speak pages'. The concepts of matching and mirroring have been around for a long time, and they are enormously powerful and the usefulness of removing unnecessary barriers and building a feeling of trust should be pretty evident. The exercises will give you an experience of this power far more than my telling you, so enjoy learning a new skill.

If you watch people who are in rapport notice how often their bodies assume the same positions, even down to eye blinks, swallowing and breathing, all NLP has done is noticed what we do when we are doing well, and made it deliberate. Have you ever been round with close friends, and although you are wide awake, if one of you yawns, the rapport is so strong the others follow suit! To take on another persons posture, breathing or tonality (matching) is the physiological equivalent of learning to speak someone else's language, and because the body affects the mind, we actually find ourselves thinking alike too, it is the closest we can get to walking in another mans shoes. Beware, however of matching or mirroring too closely someone who is depressed, unless you want to enter a disempowered state too! When Jesus stepped into our shoes in the incarnation, He did so to lift us out, not to wallow along side us!

The following exercises will get you started in matching and mirroring, so let me add two things, firstly, rapport is a dynamic process, it is a dance where you keep moving and adjusting, it isn't a static thing you attain, and secondly, after you have molded yourself to the other person for awhile (pacing) you find that when you move, they will unconsciously follow you (leading). When matching someone else, try to be inconspicuous about it, don't copy odd mannerisms, or wheeze if they have a chest complaint! There is something wonderful about a group feeling of rapport, one (only one) factor in a worship service is that we stand and sit together, we sing the same words and affirm together, but look down your row next Sunday and see how many people naturally match each other during the talk, etc. Singing together forces us to breathe at the same rate and depth, at a purely physical level can you think how powerfully this may affect those just visiting your church? if they were 'joiner inners' they would feel a part of it, if they didn't know the songs, they may feel completely out of it.

'Hands On'

– Rapport, matching and mirroring:

Initially practise with a friend until you begin to be 'unconsciously competent'. Face each other and begin a conversation, notice 'body language', breathing (location and tempo), voice tempo and tone. Begin to match or mirror, if it is difficult to see breathing, watch the shoulders rise and fall (it is not a great idea to stare at peoples chests!), and also exhale as the other person talks, and inhale when they do. Practise different accents and voice tones from TV or radio, copy tonality, pitch and tempo – you can still sound like you, but increase in flexibility and expressiveness.

– 'Total rapport':

match predicates (sensory system, see next section)

match tonality and pitch of voice

mirror breathing,

head position,

weight shifts,

placement of body parts,

hand and body movements and gestures,

body movements through space.

Representational systems:

The second main chunk of building rapport is to do with the way we think. We take in information from the outside world through our five senses, but when it comes to thinking we tend to favour or specialise in thinking in just one of the 'representational systems' we will tend to think in pictures, talk to ourselves or be a more feelings oriented 'body thinker'. We all use all systems, but tend to favour just one (much like a 'right handed person' favours that hand, but uses the other) which do you think you are? The easiest way is to listen out for the language we use, what we used to consider metaphorical language, actually seems to reflect our inner world, for example a Visual minded person may say, 'I'm looking forward to seeing you', whereas a kinaesthetic minded person would want you to 'stay in touch' while an Auditory based thinker would 'speak to you soon, or give you a ring'. A Kinesthetic thinker might not be able to 'grasp' this until it 'feels more concrete' to them. Think about each of these examples and put a V A or K next to them, I've included a taste and smell example for the sake of five senses. (V=visual, A=auditory, K=kinesthetic, O=olfactory, smell, G=gustatory, taste)

he has a colourful past	that sounds nice
a bitter pill to swallow	keep in touch
I can't quite grasp it	looks good to me
that smells fishy to me	warming to the idea
the name rings a bell	can you see the big picture?
that clicks with me	it all slots together now

Another exercise to do is to watch TV and write down all the words you hear in each category of VAKOG (or just keep a count of them), you'll be surprised at how many there are, and also notice which systems are used most and by which people. What's the point in this? imagine the following conversation …

Client: I just feel so bogged down, it's like the world is on my shoulders, it's such a drag …

Therapist: I see what you mean, let's look together and see if we can find a different perspective;

Client: I, Uh, don't feel like we're really connecting here: you don't seem to grasp how heavy all this is.

Therapist: Look, why can't you see the big picture, it's all perfectly clear to me … (etc., ad nauseam)

If we would be willing to *use the representational system of others*, it would not only increase our ability to create a feeling of rapport and being understood, but also to make us more flexible in our own thinking – many times we get stuck in our

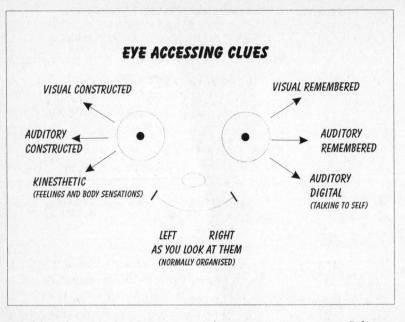

EYE ACCESSING CLUES

VISUAL CONSTRUCTED

VISUAL REMEMBERED

AUDITORY CONSTRUCTED

AUDITORY REMEMBERED

KINESTHETIC
(FEELINGS AND BODY SENSATIONS)

AUDITORY DIGITAL
(TALKING TO SELF)

LEFT   RIGHT
AS YOU LOOK AT THEM
(NORMALLY ORGANISED)

thinking because we are overusing one rep system. I know someone who is tone deaf, who believes they 'can't *carry* a tune' but if you're using the Kinaesthetic System, who can? When using rep systems, we really are speaking the same language, as well as these verbal clues, there are also 'eye-accessing cues', a person who is accessing visual information will normally have their eyes go up, or stare straight ahead defocused, an auditory thinkers' eyes will scan across horizontally, and someone accessing kinaesthetics will tend to look down, looking down may also indicate talking to oneself.

Here is a list of common phrases that identify rep systems:

Visual	Auditory	Kinaesthetic
I see your point	I hear what you're saying	That feels right to me
I take a dim view	That doesn't ring true (sound right)	It doesn't fit for me
Painting a clear picture	Is this loud and clear	Have you grasped it yet

My past is colourful	Life's in perfect harmony	Life feels warm
Future's bright	and peaceful	And comfortable

'giveaway' words:

Visual: see, look, view, appear, imagine, flash, twinkle, foggy, hazy, focused, show, reveal, sparkling, illuminate.

Auditory: hear, listen, sound, overtones, tune in / out, ring a bell, resonates, be heard, noise, silence.

Kinaesthetic: feel, touch, grasp, grip, solid, catch on, get a hold of, make contact, hard, soft, unfeeling, cold.

'Digital' or generic: think, learn, decide, know, perceive, consider, understand, experience, sense, process, compute.

Hands On

Multi-sensory language : with what we know so far, it would be possible to have (at least) three completely different descriptions of the same party, for example 'You could hardly see the other side of the room, people were dressed in the most beautiful looking outfits, the table decorations and food displays were eye-catching, it was great to see all my friends in one place.' Or how about, 'The music set a tone of celebration, and so many voices laughing and talking, what can I say? I can still hear it now,' or, 'it was such a warm time, I felt part of something bigger, it feels so good to be in touch with your friends.' It's easy to recognise the visual, auditory and kinaesthetic language in those descriptions, what do you do if you are speaking to a group? You can increase your effectiveness in communicating simply by using all three systems, you not only get your message over, the by-product is that as you develop flexibility and use in more than one favoured system, you increase your appreciation and enjoyment of the world around you too.

We can dramatically improve our communication with others with just a few of these things, use visual, auditory and kinaesthetic predicates when talking to a group, when you want to motivate someone include something to move towards and something to move away from. Listen with your eyes, pay attention and don't assume you know what the other person means just because they use a word that is familiar to you.

Constantly calibrate the emotional impact of words, and anchor positive or strong states that may be useful later in the conversation. Notice how people gesture, people will show you where they put their inner thoughts in the space around them, use those places wisely (more about this in the section on mental mapping). Finally, learn to use the word 'and' in the place of 'but' – if I said to you 'I really like you, **but** … ' the 'but' cancels out the 'really like you', If however I said 'I really like you, and I know we would get on better if …' then there is no contradiction. If we cannot agree on a subject and I say 'I understand what you are saying but …' the shutters go up, and rapport is over, Whereas if I say 'I understand what you are saying, and another way of looking at it is …' we can continue to discuss it and share our views. This one thing is far more powerful in practice than it appears on paper — go out now, do it and find out for yourself.

Metaprogrammes

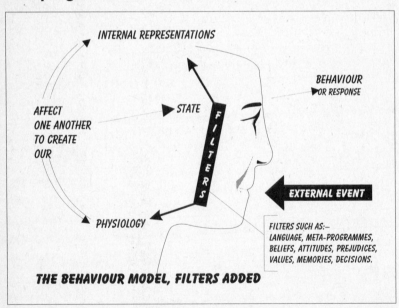

THE BEHAVIOUR MODEL, FILTERS ADDED

Another key to help us in developing rapport is understanding what lies at the back of the basic five senses, and start to add to the basic behaviour model which we have used so far, by listing the filters which are on the inside of us (see illustration):

Metaprogrammes are the most unconscious of our mental filters, because they are not about the content of what we think, but the structure – they affect they way we think about our beliefs or values. (For an excellent and comprehensive treatment of Metaprogrammes see Hall & Bodenhamer *Figuring Out People*) Metaprogrammes are context related (they may differ from a work setting to home life), and also stress related (when we are hard pressed we slip into the primary survival modes). Let's look at some examples:

moving towards
& away from
This refers to the direction of our motivation and it determines what will get us going (interestingly, it also seems to influence the whole outlook of a person) we have already thought about being motivated by pain and pleasure. Similar to this is the possibility frame, where a person looks for what *can* be done, and the necessity frame where a person looks for what *must* be done (or *can't* be done). A person with a moving towards strategy will be motivated by what is yet to come, the possibility of rewards and pleasure. A moving away from person would say that they have their head in the clouds, or are not counting the cost properly. Moving towards is a great 'get up and go' way of living, but if this person has no real goals, they will slip into inactivity – about these people Tony Robbins says, 'There are no lazy people, only those with impotent goals'. On the other hand, the moving away from strategy can be very powerful, but depends on the person's pain threshold. In a marriage where the man has a moving away from orientation, he will wait until things are really bad before he does anything about shaping up, and then after some improvement, things will be 'not too bad', the pain which motivated him will subside, and he will stop moving until the problem comes back – here we need to install a compelling vision of what marriage can be, and get leverage to keep the changes happening. Both are valid and useful strategies, both also have a downside we do well to be aware of; moving towards, may be always putting happiness and satisfaction into the future, moving away from can find itself moving just far enough, then slipping back into problems because of not following through. The Bible has examples of both, we tend to think in terms of carrot and stick, the Bible speaks in promise

and warning (Deut 28). It is a fascinating study to look at Hebrews and notice how the writer oscillates from one to the other, from terrifying warning, to glorious promise.

internal / external frames of reference Some people look outside of themselves for approval, others have a stronger sense from inside themselves, again both of these have strengths and weaknesses. It would have been no good if Paul had looked to others for approval, he would have preached an entirely different gospel (Gal 1) but instead he was motivated by his own sense of integrity and only wanted to please God. This is a great orientation in this setting, but can be a liability – have you ever met anyone who couldn't be told anything? They were always right and were not open to any new or contradictory evidence, an internal frame of reference can become pride, stubbornness and superiority if not subject to God. On the other hand as we make ourselves vulnerable and accountable to others, as we seek to live a corporate life and seek to be made whole and holy as part of the Body of Christ we are operating from an external frame of reference, this can be a strong frame for learning, receiving feedback and enjoying open relationships, but taken too far can become weak, fawning and people-pleasing. Paul in Gal 2.1-3 show the certainty Paul had, but also his willingness to be 'checked out' by the apostles in Jerusalem.

sorting by self or others Some people are strongly motivated by 'what's in it for me?' and the decisions they make can sometimes cost others a great deal, they would say a resounding 'amen' to Gal 6.4-5: 'But let each one examine his own work, and then he will have rejoicing in himself alone, and not in another. For each one shall bear his own load.' This person will take responsibility for the issues around himself, which taken too far can be old fashioned selfishness. The flipside is found in Gal 6.2: 'Bear one anothers burdens and so fulfil the law of Christ.' These people sort by others, sometimes to the detriment of themselves, mostly this is good and is serving in a Christlike way – sometimes however it is done in a 'martyrlike' way which has a hidden secondary gain, sometimes betrays low self esteem (I'm not important, don't worry about me). We are one in the Body of Christ, but we don't get lost and lose our identity, if we did, we would have nothing to contribute to everyone else.

matchers /
mismatchers ...
... or sameness and difference sorters. Someone who is a matcher will be reading this looking for what is the same as his experience, listening out for similarities and noticing if it feels right. This person is generally very easy to get along with as they want to find things in common, and to have a sense of agreement. A mismatcher will often look for the exceptions, to scan for what is wrong, or at least to find the differences in any given area. Of course, many metaprogrames function on a continuum, we are seldom one or the other, but somewhere between the two, depending on context, etc. To mismatch in a romantic relationship would not be helpful, to contradict, find exceptions and differences seldom leads to intimacy, but it is an asset in a quality control worker in a factory making precision parts, or when checking a spelling test. In the Christian walk, we see that matchers will make rapid growth early, because they are looking for all the ways that the Bible and their new-found faith are matching with their experience, they can find God anywhere! But as time progresses they may plateau if they are not willing to investigate and validate the foundations of their beliefs, and to ask harder questions about where their experience does not match with what the Bible teaches. The mismatcher, however may seem to be a pain in the neck to the people helping to disciple them, as they have 'billy goat faith' – full of buts! Nothing is left unchallenged, they seem to need to find exceptions and problems all the way, and seem to be making slow progress and be riddled with doubts, over time though, as the questions are answered, they then grow strong and certain and have a matured and 'reasonable' faith. There is no 'right' metaprogramme, but an awareness of peoples styles will help us in counselling and in meetings where decisions are made, a moving toward, matcher will be great at generating ideas, these can be developed, but then must be run by the mismatcher who will show the downside of any venture – don't involve the mismatcher too soon or it will feel as though he is pouring cold water over every new idea!

global or detail This is to do with the size 'chunks' of information that matter to you for example do you want to 'see the big picture' or 'see how it all fits together', it is important for us to learn how to chunk up and down, but normally we tend to prefer one or the other, even if it is just as a starting point. Someone who tends towards being general will feel frustrated with 'getting bogged down with detail' and the frustration can be mutual the other way as 'he never says how specifically'. We often find motivation and common ground when we chunk up, but we must also chunk down to find out the individual steps to fulfilling the 'grand vision' we are a part of!

in time / through (out of) time There are two basic orientations to time, generally speaking 'in time' people are unaware of the passage of time, of the approach of deadlines or of any need to plan or structure time, they tend to be spontaneous, easy going and 'fully in the moment', this can also mean they are frequently late and disorganised! This would reflect the time keeping of African or Arabic countries, there is a very different definition of lateness, because when you turn up, it's time to start ... maybe! 'Through time' tends to be aware of time passing (usually in a linear fashion), and are conscious of what is going to happen next, what else needs to be done, and will be structured and prepared, they also like to make lists! A 'through-time' person is not so emotionally involved in the present time but has taken a 'meta-stance' to time, separate from it to 'look on' and know how much time is left. An extreme case would be the person who when driving looks at the milometer and the speedometer and is constantly calculating and recalculating the estimated time of arrival! (More about time later, also see the excellent book *Time-Lining* by Hall & Bodenhamer).

Hands on

Metaprogrammes exercises: start to listen out for language that 'gives away' a person's metaprogrammes, also start to ask these questions with genuine interest and respect, become a metaprogramme detective:

- *moving towards or away*: ask 'why did you buy the car you have at the moment (listen for whether they tell you want they wanted or what they didn't want)

- *internal / external* frames of reference: ask 'how do you know when you've done a good job? Does someone need to tell you or do you just know?'

- for the *self / others* metaprogramme, it is easier to watch them while they are talking and when they are listening; if they lean back and seem disengaged while someone else is speaking, they probably sort by self.

- *match / mismatch*: start with 'tell me what you were doing a year ago'; if they list all the things which are the same, they are probably a matcher; if they list all the differences well, what do you think? Alternatively take out three coins, two coppers and a silver and ask them what relationship they have to each other, a matcher will describe the similarities, a mismatcher would find differences even if they were all copper!

- *global/detail*: ask 'what do you need to know before you feel ready to start a task?' if they only need the general direction or big picture they are more global-chunk oriented; if they need specific details and instructions and plans, they are more precision, small chunk minded.

- *in time / through time*: ask 'when you have time off do you plan what you will do or do you just do whatever happens?' Do you like making lists? And so on.

Personal Congruency

The final part of our practical approach to changework is that we are fully aligned with our values, with 'all parts' of ourselves. One of the things about a person with integrity is that they are so influential, that they inspire confidence, because they have a peace about themselves that makes them believable. When I talk about 'parts' I simply use a figure of speech like when we say, 'Part of me wants to go out to the cinema and part of me wants a night in', if you imagine that we have many parts that each have a positive function, one may want us to have the pleasure of company or the stimulation of a good film, another part may want us to rest as we have been working too hard, we then have 'parts in conflict' and will feel uncertain, double-minded, unsettled and anything we say on the matter will betray that incongruity to any with ears to hear. How can we increase our personal congruity? Particularly when we are thinking of helping another person I suggest we check through the following: what is our motivation for interaction with this person? Are we fed up with them or have they asked for help? Are we trying to manipulate them or help them make positive and godly changes in their life? Can we say with Jesus that we are 'aligned with the Father'? (John 5, *The Message*). Add into this the Campus Crusade for Christ motto: 'don't undertake ministry unless you are filled with the Holy Spirit', Jesus wasn't kidding when He said 'Apart from me you can do nothing', breath spiritually, make sure you are clean and full of the Holy Spirit and depending on Him. You may become skilful and be able to do a pretty good job on your own, but it will never have the life and power and touch of eternity in it, so don't short-change the people you want to help—trust the wisdom and love of the Father as well as excelling in these skills.

Hands on

Values check: ask yourself 'what is important to me about these changes?' What is important to me about helping this person?

The *6 step reframe* is an incredibly powerful technique to use on yourself or others who experience any kind of parts conflict, for example when we have mixed motivations, or a habit that they want to stop but that seems to have a life of its own, I have adapted the original 6 step reframe to go like this:

1) identify the behaviour or attitude that you would like to change,

2) thank the part of you that generates that behaviour for having produced it for you so consistently, and that it (somehow) had a positive intention for you. If you want you can ask that 'part' what the positive intention was – that can be a real surprise sometimes

3) ask that part if it would be willing to fulfil the positive intention in a different way, and then ask all other parts to help generate at least three acceptable alternative ways of meeting the positive intention – ask the Holy spirit to bring to mind any scriptures that are relevant and also imagine what Jesus – the true man – would do.

4) when that has been done check for ecology by asking, 'are there any other parts that object to incorporating these new

alternatives into my life? If there are objections then ask those parts to either modify or find different alternatives that would be OK

5) future pace, by casting your mind forward to a time when you would have generated the old unwanted behaviour, and find out how it would look, sound and feel to use one of the new alternatives, if they are still acceptable and meet the parts original intention then

6) ask the part if it would be willing to take responsibility to spontaneously and automatically provide the new acceptable behaviours in the future, wait for a feeling that tells you yes, if you get a 'no' cycle back through steps 3 – 5 until you do.

> [This may sound a little weird, but it is a very effective and powerful way of communicating with our unconscious, and ridding ourselves of conflicts and problem behaviours that we couldn't previously deal with by just 'trying']

Four categories of behaviour

Before going on to the next chapter, let's learn a diagnostic tool to apply to change in your own life, and others lives too. There are four categories of behaviour:

– *Feels good, is good for you,* or others, or is consistent with being a Christian. This is the kind of behaviour we do not need to change, and is, in one sense, the ideal for us, when something we say or do, is good for us or others and consistent with the Bible and God's will for our lives AND feels good – these are areas of our lives where we are moving in the right direction

– *Feels good, is bad for you,* or others, or is inconsistent with being a Christian. These are some of the most destructive behaviours of all, because we sometimes feel powerless to tackle them (we will not only understand why this is, but also how to gain power over them in a later chapter), we can all think of times when rationally we know something is harmful, or inconsistent, but we do it anyway – and then pay, and pay, and pay!

– *Feels bad, is good for you,* or others, or is consistent with being a Christian. This is one category that it is worth paying attention to, later in the book we will see how to not only motivate ourselves to do things we know we should do, and must be done but in the short term seem unpleasant or boring, but also how various martyrs in church history have 'taken pleasure' in suffering and persecution – this is a very Biblical skill (see Matt 5 v.10-12, and Acts 5 v.41, etc.)

– *Feels bad, is bad for you,* or others, or is inconsistent with you being a Christian. Of course, this is one category of behaviour we usually find it easy to avoid, the exception being those who deliberately hurt and damage themselves, and even attempt suicide – you will see in a later chapter that because of the mental and emotional associations this person has made, that they would not label destructive behaviour as a category 4 at all.

'Hands On'

- Go through your own experience and make a list of several behaviours that fit into each of the four categories.

- Spend some time thinking about what you have to think about or ignore, and how you represent those thoughts, in order to persist in a category 2 behaviour (feels good, is bad), and also what you are not aware of when struggling to take up a category 3 behaviour (feels bad, is good).

Answers to sensory acuity quiz:

1) Mindread, 2) Mindread, 3) Sensory specific, 4) Mindread, 5) Sensory specific, 6) Sensory specific, 7) Mindread, 8) Sensory specific, 9) Mindread, unless he had a very peculiar tattoo!, 10) Sensory specific, although flinched can be used in an emotionally charged fashion and imply more than the action.

Chapter 7

Modelling Jesus, the modelling process

So what does a person need to know in order to model effectively? We need to learn 'what is the difference that makes the difference?' I remember as a young man having a Bible teacher who was a real hero to me. I wanted to have his knowledge, his intimate walk with God and his ability to present profound truth clearly, so I listened to hundreds of hours of tapes, read his books and went to see him at every opportunity. Over time I found that I was learning a great deal about the Bible, and my spiritual life was developing, but a close friend pointed out that I was also using this man's mannerisms and idiosyncrasies and they were off-putting and came across as phoney. I have had others copy my way of dressing and certain phrases because they have wanted to be like me in some other way.

In the modelling process we have an objective position, we know what skills, attributes and characteristics we want to model and are able to focus on those. For example, if I want to learn to ski, I only want to learn skiing skills from my tutor, I am not interested in his personal relationships at all. We are surrounded in life with a rich reserve of experience, insight and skill, and can be selective in how much we receive from the people we model – my driving instructor was full of ideas about how a young man (as I was then) would want to spend his time and money, fortunately to drive well I didn't need to take his values on board! As we approach modelling Jesus we can exercise a little less restraint, although not everyone would want to wear sandals and a robe or grow a beard (especially the ladies!).

NLP has developed specific ways to accelerate the modelling process. We do not need to start from scratch in our apprenticeship – this is presupposed in every Christian book and discipleship course, that we can learn from another's experience – if we repeat exactly what the other person does both inside and outside, we stand a good chance of appropriating their skills – or at least having a head start in knowing what questions to ask next. NLP is able to take the concept of 'What would Jesus do' and take it out of the abstract into something you can really use and develop in your life, WWJD is a basic approach to modelling and imitating Christ.

The first stage is to *know what you want to model*, and make sure you have found someone worth modelling, if you had problems in your relationships there would be no point in modelling someone else whose results in relationships are even worse—we must look for excellence! Success leaves clues and Jesus is the most excellent person in human history. Having defined what we want to model, and selected a person to model, we then have to pay attention to what the person does, *watch closely*, observe, notice firstly the behaviours, what are they doing? Notice it all, then ask about what do they believe to be able to do that? What's important to them? what do they have to believe about other things that supports them being excellent at it? Only then ask about how they do things, and not just listening to what they say, notice what they do with their voice tone, their breathing, their gestures and posture – often when people are speaking they are demonstrating what is happening in their mind, we need to learn to pay attention to this, listen also for figures of speech which can be taken literally, you will notice this more as we work through this book.

The next step is a matter of *mapping out the order and sequence* of what the person does in their head and body, and then starting to try it on to find out what is essential and what is not essential, an interesting part of this process can be to use the 'as if' frame best illustrated by a story in *The Inner Game of Skiing* by T. Gallwey, he asked a woman to demonstrate how a famous and accomplished skier would tackle a particular slope that she was fearful of trying, she set off and did the slope successfully, and then said, 'That's how he would do it, but of course I couldn't do that!' (p.77). Sometimes we are able to 'just pretend' for the sake of learning, all children do it as they play Mums and Dads – of course we need to realise that acting 'as if' we have a skill for the sake of enhancing our learning is different to actually having the fully developed skill, we want our confidence to match our competence, I wouldn't want a surgeon who was only acting as if they knew what they were doing!

A lovely metaphor for learning to model and imitate Jesus is that of learning language: a small child has an inbuilt desire and need to communicate, and the attention is on communication, not on the actual language itself, add to this that a child learns in a safe and supportive environment from members of its family, that every noise and attempt at speaking was encouraged and reinforced with 'coos' and 'Ahs' – not endlessly corrected. A child learns by trial and error until it is understood, it doesn't try once or twice and then 'know' within itself that this speaking thing is just not for them! A child very quickly is able to recognise an ill-formed sentence, even appreciate puns and word plays (most 'knock, knock' jokes) fortunately as children we did not have to learn grammar, syntax and regular verbs before we were allowed to speak. As followers of Jesus Christ, it is natural for us to grow like Jesus, hopefully our churches and Christian friendships are supportive, encouraging and don't judge us for trying and failing, one of the most powerful things in helping a new Christian grow is to get excited about every step in the right direction – Jesus didn't expect his disciples to have all the answers before he let them loose on the world, nor should we.

If you wanted to make a cake but had no experience at baking, rather than just muddling along, you could rapidly increase your chances of success by getting a good recipe book thereby modelling someone who can already bake, this would give you their *strategy*. So what does a recipe give you? Firstly, the ingredients, sugar, flour, milk, eggs, etc. In modelling a persons behaviour *the ingredients will be what they do in their minds, and what they do with their bodies.* There are actually a limited number of ingredients in human experience, our five senses seeing, hearing, feeling, smelling, tasting, and whether what we see, hear, feel is outside our bodies in the world, our represented to us in our mind. In NLP the sense systems are written as Visual (V), Auditory (A), Kinaesthetic (feeling, K), Olfactory (smell O), Gustatory (taste G), with an accompanying 'E' for external, in the world outside, or 'I' for internal, inside our minds. So to know how another person does something we want to model and learn, first we must find out what they do, this will often be more complex than a simple stimulus-response link, and will be a more complex 'chain reaction', although often triggered by an initial stimulus. So in our recipe, we want to know what order and sequence to handle the ingredients, for example we might have the right digits in a telephone number but if we mix up the sequence we will never get through. To get motivated to do something a person may see the untidy room (visual external Ve), say something to themselves (auditory internal Ai), and feel motivated (K), as a strategy this would be written Ve Ai K, they might never get round to it if they never noticed, or only ever talked to themselves. This is a good start, but there is a bit more to a recipe – the specific amounts and qualities of the ingredients. In each representational system (our five senses) there are detailed distinctions we can make, for example, if we have an internal image, is it black and white, or colour? A movie or still frame? What is its location – centre, left, right, up down? Is it near or far etc? With sounds we would ask about volume, rhythm, tempo, location, also if the person said something to themselves we want to know what they said and the way they said it, etc. Once we had got a list not just of the ingredients, but also of the specific amounts, qualities and order, then we would try out the 'recipe', first with the person we learned it from, to see whether it worked for them, them with ourselves to find out if we could replicate their results, and finally if that was successful we could teach it to other people and share the joy of a new recipe.

To discover a persons *strategy* we need simply to ask some simple questions and pay attention to the answers, first we need to help the person remember vividly and fully the time they did the thing we want to know about for example, if I was asking about learning it could go something like this:

- Think of a time when you were able to learn something quickly and easily, think of a specific time ... (wait until the person has a specific time)

- How do you know it's time to begin learning, do you see something, hear something or feel something? What is the very first thing?

- After you {saw | heard | felt}, what was the very next thing that caused you to be totally able to learn quickly and easily? Did you make a picture in your mind? Say something to yourself? Have a certain feeling or emotion? What was the very next thing?

  [Keep cycling through this until you reach the point where the person has learned something (or whatever you are eliciting – excitement, motivation, determination, confidence etc.)]

- Then go back and check the sequence with the person, if it is right, then for each step, ask about the *specific qualities* of the pictures, sounds, words and feelings, and then test it out on the person.

It is useful to remember the ***TOTE*** model when dealing with strategies. A strategy has a particular result or outcome as its end, there is often something that triggers the start of the strategy, and the various elements running through are parallel to the operate, test sections until there is the final point where the strategy and the TOTE exit. This would have to do with knowing when the cake was cooked, we need to know when it's done or we will have burnt offerings again and again. With this in mind, look out for any repeating loops in a strategy for example if a person looks at a thing and talks to themselves about it repeatedly before acting on it we can streamline the repetition out of the strategy.

When we have got the recipe of a master chef, it may have taken them years of trial and error, but we can reduce our learning time down to weeks or even days, it is good for us to learn how to use strategies because then we can consistently duplicate good results we are already getting, also to help other people too, and most importantly we have a way of starting to model excellence in others and in Christ.

Whole books have been written about strategies – how to elicit them and use them in daily life, strategies for accelerated learning, spelling, negotiating, etc., my purpose here is to alert you to the possibility of a person even inadvertently telling you how they accomplish certain results – the Bible is full of examples, the Psalms in particular where the psalmist will speak to himself, look out at creation, recall acts of God in both word and image and then feel joy, gratitude and trust – this can help us approach scripture with 'new eyes' to learn that God even understands and teaches subjective experience. We all have strategies for anything that we do more than once, whether the result is love, joy and peace or anger, disappointment, stress and depression. The Bible teaches us how to update and enhance our strategies to include how to forgive, to manage our time, finances and emotions, and how to think, feel and behave more and more like Jesus. The chances are that until now, the strategies you have that work for you have been out of consciousness and you had to just hope that some environmental trigger would fire you off in the right direction, now you are able to be more deliberate about what states and results you experience.

Another factor in modelling that overlays the strategies we have elicited is that as human beings we function on different *'logical levels'*. As we read the gospels it becomes apparent very quickly that Jesus was not random in His ministry, just 'going with the flow' but rather had clear goals (as we should too) for example Luke 4.18ff to preach the good news, to heal, to set prisoners free, to establish God's Kingdom, to do Hid Father's will, to seek the lost sheep (Matt 10.6), etc. If we were modelling Jesus only on the level of *environment*, then we would all have to go to Israel to grow spiritually which would be ridiculous, but what we can model concerning environment is that Jesus made sure He was with the sick, needy and sinful, He was even criticised for eating and drinking with them. If we have goals, then we need to know where we need to be in order for us to have the chance to act. Next level up we come to *behaviours* which is where we see Jesus' goals translated into tangible actions, He called His disciples, He taught the multitudes, He touched the lepers and sick, etc. Again if we modelled only behaviours we could end up smearing mud on blind peoples eyes, and cursing fig trees – there may be a time for these things, but it becomes apparent that just mimicry at lower logical levels with no understanding of the person behind them will not gain the results we want. At the level of *capabilities*, Jesus seems to operate from the principle that whatever He sees the Father doing or hears the Father saying, He can do and say – similarly with us we can do all things through Christ who strengthens us (Phil 4.13) and apart from Him we can do nothing (John 15.5) we have the capability to obey and do what we are told to do in scripture, no more, no less – whether we act on those capabilities is a question of our will, not our potential.

Stepping up another logical level we can see that Jesus' *rules and values* were in conflict with those of the leading Jews, they had ideas about the Messiah (rules) that did not match with how Jesus behaved, therefore they 'knew' He wasn't the one, Jesus' rules about whether a person was 'right' had more to do with whether they did the will of God (not whether they could wax lyrical about it), and according to hid primary rule which was love. Jesus also operated from and taught His *beliefs* for example, there is only One God (Matt 4.10), who is a loving, merciful creator (Matt 6.1-34, Luke 15.11-32). He believed that people are valuable, can change, need liberating and are children of God (Matt 5.21-26, 4.19, 7.7-11, 9.36). It is worth adding the following list of Jesus' values to your life, and dumping any that contradict them, the values that drove Jesus' life and ministry were: God's will (Jn 3.34), people (Jn 10.14-15), love (Matt 5.43-48), Mercy (Matt 5.7), Joy (Luke 10.21), peace (Jn 14.1), gentleness (Matt 5.4), freedom (Jn 8.36), forgiveness (Matt 5.12,14-15) and salvation (Matt 7.13-14). If we take these on board as the criteria by which we judge whether a thing is good, bad, worthwhile or not, we will find ourselves thinking with the mind of Christ and acting in ways that show His character in us. If we live in accordance with our values we will feel whole and fulfilled whatever our outward circumstances (Phil 4.12) if we violate our values we will feel acute personal pain, no matter how good our life looks to others. Our values are able to produce pleasure at different logical levels, for example moral and spiritual values may not be comfortable at the environmental levels (because we may go to people who are sick and in need or not be able to indulge in self gratifying behaviours) but will bring us joy at the higher levels, Jesus even taught this as a skill in the sermon on the mount, to be able to rejoice and be glad in being persecuted for Jesus' sake, this is the power of values in our experience. Our values (what we evaluate as important or not) are what motivate us before we do a thing, and also are how we evaluate after the fact. Our values give our life meaning, if we set goals without knowing why they are important to us, we may accomplish them and then think 'is that all there is?' Our values are central to our happiness and growth. To be able to imitate Christ, we must let the transformation take place from the inside out.

• Strategies give us the way to begin modelling behaviours, to begin to *model beliefs* we must first discover what they are and how they relate to one another, we can do this by asking simple questions, imagine yourself as one of the disciples asking Jesus these questions at the end of a days teaching and healing – what do you think He would answer?

• Why do you do what you do?

• What does that mean to you?

• What would happen if you didn't do that?

• What is that like? What do you compare it to? (Jesus loved comparing things, that's what a parable is)

• What is empowering / important to you about this

Then compare these answers with what you already believe, what new actions would you make if you believed that? What would you differently? What would you stop doing? What else would you be capable of?

Doesn't it suddenly get exciting? You are getting to the heart of the matter, knowing why your life is the way it is and how God is starting to highlight things that He now wants to change so you are more like Jesus.

Finally *the highest logical level is that of our identity and union with God* (NLP usually does not make much of the spiritual dimension of our identity, but we can) Jesus was fully able to do what he did, and value what he did, because He knew who he was – even to the extent of washing his disciples' feet, he could do this because he was secure in who he was. Likewise, while we could never be The Son of God, we have been made children of God (John 1.12-14) and nothing can separate us from His love (Rom 8.28-39) and so the process of us becoming like

Jesus can take place. We also learn at this highest level that there are certain attitudes of Jesus that are above environment, behaviour, capability and even belief, things that Jesus *is*, congruency (integrated wholeness), acceptance and empathy are more than techniques. If, like Jesus, you are congruent, accepting and empathetic it will affect what you believe about other people, and make you capable of reaching out in new ways to perform behaviours and actions which will touch and transform not just the people you meet but your environment as well. When we think, about identity we mean it to describe who we are, as a description of our very being, sometimes in our thinking and speaking we get logical levels confused, for example if a Mother tells her child, 'You are stupid', she is making a statement about the child's identity, in actuality she is confusing the logical levels – maybe her child made a mistake at homework or knocked something over, these would belong to the level of behaviours, not identity! NLP has taught us that *we seldom, if ever solve a problem on the same logical level,* normally we need to move up a level – Saul of Tarsus was stopped from persecuting the church by a complete change in identity, not by simply changing his actions – it is this insight that gives us confidence that there is no problem too great for us, because we have a living relationship with the One who is above all logical levels, who is Ultimate reality, and who can do all things.

Another piece to modelling is what *perspective* we view a behaviour from, for example, if you take the account of Jesus' feet being anointed by a sinful woman in Luke 7.36-50: if you were the woman then from the *first perspective* you would slip into the room where Jesus was eating, glance around and see who else was there, and then go to Jesus' feet, kneel down weeping and begin to anoint his feet. You would be acutely aware of the fact that some of the people knew you were a sinful woman, how would you feel? What would you say to yourself? You would hear the discussion between Simon and Jesus, and eventually hear Jesus say to you, 'Your faith has saved you, go in peace'.

From a *second perceptual position* however, say through Jesus' eyes, you would see the woman lurking in the shadows, then coming forward, already weeping, and start to wet your feet with her tears. You would look at not just her appearance, but inside her heart, at the love and hope and pain, you would be moved with love and compassion toward her. You would hear Simons' criticism of her and use the opportunity to teach him about your values, finally you declare her saved by her faith.

From a *third perceptual position*, say Simon's, it is different again, imagine yours shame and horror at that type of woman gaining entry into your house when you have this new Rabbi visiting, how do you feel as he reads your thoughts and tells you this barbed story? Can you believe it that he forgives her?

An *alternative third perspective* would be an uninvolved bystander, as an observer you gain a lot of insight without being involved emotionally. Finally of course there is God's perspective, as he looks on, how does he feel about the woman? His Son? Simon the Pharisee? What things does he say about each person and their interactions, how do they fit into His 'big picture?'

In the film *Prince of Egypt* about the life of Moses, one of the key learning experiences for him is when Jethro sings the song 'Look at your life through Heavens eyes', often as Christians we run to the pages of Scripture to give meaning and a new perspective on our lives, both successes and failures. Paul talks about how from one perspective he was the best Pharisee ever, but from his own, having glimpsed Gods love, he now considers it dung (Phil 3.2-15) he says that all of us that are mature should have 'this view', God's view. While this will be dealt with more thoroughly later, try this experiment:

From your own perspective (first position) open yourself to God, approach Him and notice what you see, say, think and feel as you come to Jesus, take a moment as you would when beginning to pray. Now in your minds eye, step into Jesus' shoes, look back at yourself through His eyes, how would he be feeling as you come to Him in prayer? How does he look at you? What does he say about you, what does he believe about you? Then float off into the position of an observer, look over there at Jesus and you, look and listen to the interaction, how does Jesus speak to you over there? How do you respond to him? as you watch it happen as if to someone else, what sort of impression does it leave you with? Now come back into first position and look again with your own eyes, keeping the learnings of how you appear to Jesus and also to an observer … Useful isn't it? When I first did this exercise I realised that I didn't let Jesus get a word in edgeways, and that from his perspective there were many answers he longed to give me, and many things he wanted to share with me, from an observers point of view the whole interaction looked almost comical, with me coming in, dumping all my concerns and rushing out before Jesus could deal with me. Rather than beat myself up, I then went to Jesus and let him talk, a blessed relief for both of us!

As you read the Bible it is fascinating to notice how language shifts from one person to another, prophecy is written when a person assumes second position and allows God to speak through them (in the first person), many of the Psalms are written in third position, talking about 'His mighty acts' and then switching to first position, 'stepping into' those things and responding, 'Your love O Lord reaches to the heavens, etc.'. As an exercise, look at Psalm 104, notice how it switches from first position (associated) saying 'you' to third position (dissociated) 'He' and then back again, this builds an attitude of faith and praise and gratitude in the psalmist, which if we would copy would produce the same result in us. If you look in Psalm 91 you find that this moving perceptual positions happens again, even to the extent that the last three verses are God speaking through the psalmist!

If we always sing hymns and songs about God as 'He' we will have what feels like an observers faith, it could seem distant, abstract or historical – it is real but not tangible, the Bible is about what happens to 'other people', whereas when we sing to 'You' in our praise, God seems more immediate and more present. The strength of the third position is that we develop a good objective understanding of God and His dealings with humanity, the strength of the first position is that we personalise and associate into those objective truths and know God's love as personal as well as universal, the value of second position with Jesus is that we gain insight, and wisdom simply by recognising that He is calm and still in charge!

Shifting perceptual positions is often a useful thing for parents to do if they have a child who is causing them grief. If you were to remember an incident with your child, from first position you would see what they had done, also feel how you feel about it, hear yourself maybe telling them off and experience the whole 'movie' from your point of view. Now stop, float out of your body to second position, your child – what do you see now? What did you think you were doing? how do you feel as you look up at this big grown up shouting down at you? What do you want to tell them that they just won't hear? What's going on inside of you that they don't know about? How does that feel? Now stop again, float out of your body to a third position, a detached observer, looking on as if it were two other people over there, what do you see? Hear? Look at the way the parent and child are using their bodies, how do you feel about it as you watch from a distance? Now stop and float back into first position, look down at your child, have you gained any insight from this exercise? Would you do things differently? Do you need to learn something, even to apologise? Many parents find this a powerful experience with challenging children, also husbands and wives, bosses and employees who feel that the 'other person' just isn't 'getting it', run through this exercise and find out how much you were missing. This is also useful for when we are planning a negotiation, to think of the matter from all perspectives rather than just our own, I also use it automatically when I am preparing a talk: I experience it from different people's viewpoints to find out if it is clear and also whether an illustration is appropriate.

So, *to model a person or a behaviour we have to put all these things together;* we want to know about the environment, the specific behaviours, and the strategy that is used to produce them, then to know the driving beliefs, values and identity, as well as the goals (TOTEs) and perspectives that the person operates from. As we think about how to help another person change, we can use these distinctions to find out how they create depression, stress, unhappiness, etc. and have a good idea of how to intervene and also at what logical level to create the best, long-lasting changes. God has given us an abundant source of material in the Bible, NLP and modelling can actually give us a new and practical hermeneutic (way of studying and interpreting the Bible) where we start to notice all kinds of important details that help us 'crack the code' in modelling Jesus.

Chapter 8

The Power of Words

Do you believe the children's rhyme that says 'sticks and stones may break my bones, but words will never hurt me'? Do you believe that 'talk is cheap'? Or have you, like me, found that some words have the ability to go 'down into the innermost parts'? That 'Death and life are in the power of the tongue' (Prov 18.18). Language is of primary importance to us as human beings, it is more than only words, it is the whole experience of communication, but words play an enormous part in it. When we have good communication, we have good relationships, we may not agree with everyone, but we do at least have a degree of understanding. This chapter is about making sure we understand what we mean, and then say what we mean, also to understand what other people mean and make sure they understand what they mean! In essence it is about reconnecting our language with experience, this is where we learn some of the 'linguistics' that can programme and direct us to feel and behave the way we do consistently. Wars have been started and terrible events have taken place because of careless words or misunderstandings, things have been done that should never have happened and others left undone that were of the utmost importance. Words are so important, and precision in our language can transform our experience and that of those around us. Another area I invite you to bear in mind is the way you pray, apply some of the following distinctions to your communication with God, and enjoy the results. As we learn to really hear what a person is saying, we are able to 'get inside' their map of the world either to learn and model them, or to know where the map is distorted or corrupted and needs updating.

The process of language: you remember that 'out there' is true, objective reality, and that through our senses and unconscious filters we take in information. This level of experience is called the 'deep structure', and there is a lot to it, when we re-present it to ourselves internally. There is a fair amount of information that is lost, we then 'language' it to ourselves. Finally if we want to transmit it to someone else, we use our (limited) vocabulary and present to the other person the 'surface structure' in the form of a string of words. Our words are doubly removed from reality, and there is a lot of scope for corruption, we give words their meaning from anchored associations through our life and experience, words are anchors for the sensory experiences we have, also for the meanings we overlay on them, but our experience is not the reality, and the word is not the experience! It has been said that arguing about the meaning of a word is like arguing that one menu tastes better than another because you prefer the food that is printed on it! Michael Hall says, 'If you operate from a set of linguistics that inaccurately map reality or that are toxic in nature, you will find yourself less and less able to effectively navigate human reality and more and more sick with certain kinds of thoughts and emotions – this is the power of your linguistic – semantic reality, it makes life a heaven or a hell.' Add into this that as anchors, they can evoke good and bad states, and therefore affect our quality of life and behaviour. Seymour[5] says, 'What happens to our thoughts as we clothe them in language, and how faithfully are they preserved when our listeners undress them?'

The 'filtering process' Richard Bandler and John Grinder noticed that while the speaker would have a full representation of what he wanted to say (the deep structure) in order to not take forever in communicating it, the deep structure would go through (at least) three processes to become the sentence (surface structure), these three processes are out of our conscious awareness until we begin to use the 'meta-model' (meta is a Greek word for 'over, on a different level' therefore the meta-model uses language at a higher level to clarify the words and language on a lower level, it deals with the structure of the language, not getting caught up with the content). The three process are as follows: firstly, because there is so much information at the deep level, we have to *select* what to include, this means by implication a lot will be left out, or *deleted*. Secondly, we have to *simplify* our version, so it will inevitably become *distorted*. Finally, to avoid having to go through all possible exceptions we will *generalise*. No wonder sometimes we are presented with a 'fuzzy surface structure' where we really don't know what it is the other person has in mind, I have a co-worker often uses the word 'stuff' – he might say. 'We went to the meeting and worshipped and stuff.' To me 'stuff' could mean prayed quietly, to someone else it may mean cast out demons and raised the dead, but my friend meant that they stood around talking and having a laugh afterward! This example wouldn't matter too much, but think of the possibilities … Let's go through some of the most common language violations and see how enormously practical this can be.

The wonderful world of words

Let's turn our attention first of all to *deletions* – where for the sake of including only what we think is relevant, other information is left out too:

Level one

The first category of information that can be dropped from a sentence is *who or what the sentence is about*; that's easily done because of course *we* know who we are talking about, and assume that any intelligent listener would too! (In neuro-linguistics this is called the 'unspecified noun or referential index') Neil Anderson[6] tells a story in *Rivers of Revival* that highlights how powerful this deletion can be: 'The board meeting was not going as I hoped it would. Anybody who had a modicum of discernment could sense the tension in the air. Then one of the old charter members of the church said, "Well, people are saying …" Before he could continue, I asked "Who's saying that, Jim?," "Well, I would rather not say," he answered. "Then I would rather not hear," I responded, "because it makes all the difference in the world who is saying it." I knew he was the only one saying it, so he withdrew the statement. This was another frustrating moment of subtle intimidation and game playing with the leaders of the church.'

Can you imagine how powerful it feels when 'people' are saying something? You don't know who they are so you can't check your facts, can't put relationships right or challenge any inaccuracies, but knowing that 'they' are against you can crush your spirit flat.

Whenever we replace the name of a person or an object with words like, he, she, it, they, some people, other people, etc. we have lost information that is vital to know. To recover what was lost, we only need to ask *'who or what, specifically?'* Get some practice with these examples:

'They don't like me' (who specifically?), 'It's not going to work' (what specifically?), 'People never listen to me', 'Nobody likes me', They never come on time',
'I didn't like it', 'This is stupid', 'People are really selfish', 'Other people do it' [there's two here].

Level two

The next deletion is where a word is used to describe *an action, set of events or a process*, but so much is left out we can't think clearly what is meant, for example, if I tell you 'She hurt me' (first find out 'who specifically'), you don't know whether she shot me in the foot, ignored me in the street or called me a name I didn't like! To recover the lost information we need only ask *'How specifically* (did she hurt you)?' In church circles again, there can be some fascinating deletions; 'I tested this guidance', 'God demonstrated His power in the meeting', 'He really worshipped' 'We offered the sacrifice of praise' (come on, 'how specifically?'). More practice:

'She helped me', 'I travelled to London', 'That upset me', 'It concerns us' — Notice how deletions can be 'stacked' and seem meaningful, but you have no idea of 'what' or 'how'.

Level three

A slightly more subtle form of deletion is when we hear a statement with a *comparison or judgement* in it, words like 'good, better, best, worst, more, less, bad, badly'. We don't know what it is compared to or who is making the comparison. There is an immediate relevance in terms of Satan's accusation and feelings of failure, we hear our doubts telling us we are no good, or our pride saying that we are good, but such comments do not exist in a vacuum. Firstly we must ask *'compared to what?'*, and secondly, *'according to whom?'*

With our behaviour, our only benchmark is Jesus, never another person (see Matt 7.1ff), but what about other comparisons? 'new stain-shift is better' (compared to what? – it may be better than coal dust , but what are we comparing it to?), or 'I handled that complaint badly' badly compared to what? Compared to Attila the Hun, Superman? Mother Theresa? The other challenge is 'according to whom?', sometimes we make a value judgement or statement and forget we are saying it, it then sounds like an absolute truth 'This is the best way to worship' sounds different to 'I think that this is the best way to worship', this is also called the 'lost performative' – the person performing the judgement or pronouncing a judgement is lost, so not only do *they* forget they are saying it, it lets us think *we* are saying it! Satan has had a field day with this one. When we recover the lost information of 'according to whom' we can decide whether we want to take the statement on board, after all, 'if God be for us, who can be against us, and who will gainsay God?' Start to notice how many comparisons cross your path over the next few days:

'He is the best in the class', 'That was a bad thing to do', 'It's good to go and see them', 'You make me feel better', 'That's stupid', 'It's wrong that boys should cry'

Also look out for words like 'obviously', 'clearly', 'it is apparent': if you are told 'Obviously he is a high achiever', it is worth asking, 'Obvious to whom?' Many dubious presuppositions can sneak in behind such 'obvious' words!

Level four

There is a fascinating group of words known as *'nominalisations'* – which is when a verb (action-word) becomes a noun (thing-word), examples are decision, respect, communication, relationship, fear and education. The standard NLP test is 'can you put it in a wheelbarrow?' If it is a true noun, a person or a thing you will be able to, if it is actually a process or action that has been *'thingyfied'*, you have an empty wheelbarrow. The other test suggested by Michael Hall is to fit it into the sentence 'An ongoing _____ ' a nominalisation will make sense (like relationship or fear) a true noun will not (like an ongoing table or John). Before going on to the meta-model challenge let's consider how nominalisations can disempower us.

A very unhappy man came to see me about his working life. As we spoke he said, 'Well the decision has been made,' and then described how he had no choices but to leave, or take a significant drop in income. As he spoke he gestured to his right as if pointing to this decision as if it was a thing on the sofa beside him. I started to ask him, 'Who was doing the deciding? What information did they use in the decision process? How did they go about deciding one thing rather than another?' In answering these and other similar questions he started to turn this intangible and immovable 'thing' back into a process – a process that wasn't over yet, he recovered the information of who was deciding, how they were deciding and what information he hadn't yet given that would change the outcome. On top of that we then discovered that he had taken a tentative suggestion (another nominalisation) as if it was a decision, and had felt powerless to do anything about it!

Another example is when I see couples for marriage counselling, I am told 'we have trouble in our relationship, it's a communication problem.' A relationship is an ongoing process of relating to one another, communication is the process of communicating with one another, when we *turn these 'things' back into actions*, the couples are able to see how changing their responses and behaviour is done; it is hard to change a 'thing-like' relationship, because you can't even find it! When we denominalise these words back into actions, the person recovers their role in the process and are then empowered to take responsibility and action to change it.

Many emotionally charged words are nominalisations, they often represent states of emotion or being to us, they are used by politicians and gurus to evoke feelings in their hearers, they are offered to us as things, but actually are not, they are verbs. The Church has a good share in the nominalisation market, worship is described as a thing, so is prayer, salvation is the action of being saved, and the state of being saved, but is offered as if from a wheelbarrow. I personally believe 'Christian' is a nominalisation, or at least a 'nominal Christian' is someone who should be in the process of being saved, who has turned into a static and intangible thing! – I say this only half in jest.

The meta-model challenge is simply to take this 'thing' and *turn it back into a verb, into a process,* try these on for size:

'Our friendship is in difficulty', 'It was a strange sensation', 'We had a communication breakdown', 'He has a powerful ministry'

The next group of language patterns that can limit our lives and cause no end of confusion are *generalisations.* The process of generalising is part of the way we learn, if we didn't do it, we would have to learn how to open each door we ever encountered, rather than learning from the experience of our first doors, and generalising from that, so we can enter a new room without even thinking about it. When we generalise, we streamline our thinking, and make a 'this is like that' connection – our minds compare and associate new data with similar old data. Fortunately the world is not so dull and uniform that a few experiences of a thing give us the full idea of it, unfortunately we can hold our generalisations in spite of new information and end up in an unreal and limited world – our map is faulty and our decisions and behaviour will reflect these limitations. In one sense, generalisations are the language of our faith, because they betray our beliefs, about what is possible, impossible, necessary and many of our 'global' beliefs – they describe the size of your world. For example when we think of something as impossible we tend to give up, to avoid the additional pain of disappointment, but who is a candidate for a miracle? Only the person who has no possible, natural solutions to their problem! God waited until Abraham's body was as good as dead before He performed the miracle of Isaac's birth, because if He hadn't, we wouldn't have known it was a miracle! As you go through these sections, remember that God transcends our thinking about Him.

Level five

One of the most common (and often frustrating) mindsets you will encounter when helping people make positive changes is expressed in a 'modal operators of possibility' (the mode we operate in the world, do we function from a world of laws, and therefore necessity, or from opportunities and therefore possibility?) – words like *'can, can't, possible, impossible, am, am not, will, will not'*. Before I learned the meta-model I used to use the 'Rhino' approach to 'can't' where I would charge at it with the full force of my personality and say 'of course you can!', and of course I would lose rapport, and cognitive dissonance would click in and I would feel they were either being stupid or stubborn – neither of which put me at my most resourceful! Fritz Perls, founder of Gestalt therapy, used to insist, 'Don't say I can't, say I won't' – while this was good in moving the client to a position of choice (and therefore at cause, not effect) often people find this presupposition too great a jump to make.

Now, there are some things that are impossible, that can't be done – we can't live without oxygen, we couldn't approach a holy God without the covering blood of Christ, but when we say, 'I just can't speak to him,' or, 'I can't believe God can forgive me,' we are stating our limiting beliefs which do not correspond with reality. The meta-model challenge for can'ts and such like is *'What prevents you?'*, this gives us information as to what generalisations and beliefs are at work 'behind the scenes', sometimes there is a real barrier, most often the person will 'go inside' and bring back a belief. The meta-model is a great tool for deconstructing a false belief, (as are the 'doubt creating' questions found in the 'beliefs' section of the behaviour model).

'I can't go to Church',   'I can't change my beliefs',
'Its impossible to believe in the resurrection',
'I can't stop smoking'

Level Six

For the person whose world is full of laws, we detect the limitations of their map of the world by hearing 'modal operators of necessity', words like *'must, must not, ought, should and need to.'* These are a great source of inflicting guilt on ourselves and on others. They state a rule, and of course, when we break a rule we feel guilt, many of the 'shoulds' we encounter come from our own imagination, rather than God's Word, and therefore produce false guilt. Another thing we do is look back with hindsight and say 'I should have done X and Y …' we then manage to impose broken rules and guilt on ourselves retrospectively – how wonderful we are! The challenge to these words is

'What would happen if you did / didn't?' For example, 'I ought to go and visit so and so', 'well, what would happen if you didn't?', what would happen if you did?' this connects up the speaker with reality again, and if there is a legitimate reason, then they can be clear on it, but most often answering this question either frees them from false duty and guilt or highlights an erroneous belief which can be dealt with.

'I must always eat what's on my plate', 'I shouldn't have come here', I ought to go and see the Pastor', 'We really should talk to him about it', 'You have to use this version of the Bible'.

Level Seven

One of my favourite kinds of generalisations are 'universal quantifiers', these are words with a global, all inclusive scope, like *'All, every, never, always, none'*. Some universals are true: all have sinned and fallen short of God's glory; night always follows day. But when we make a statement that gives no room for exceptions, although it sounds like a 'big' statement, it actually limits our experience, because it becomes an unconscious filter that prevents us from seeing the exceptions. For a person to believe they always get things wrong, they have to delete or disregard every instance when things went well. There are two ways to challenge universals, firstly just *repeat it back in a questioning tone of voice,* e.g. 'You never listen to me', 'what, <u>never</u>?', this can been humorous and respectful an get them to retrieve counterexamples to the belief 'well, you do listen <u>sometimes</u>', this is a way of making the person's map more accurate and therefore their responses more appropriate. Similarly you could ask *'has there ever been a time when ...'* and ask for a counterexample, when there was an *exception* or when the opposite was true. The second way of challenging universals was developed by Frank Farelly[7] in *Provocative Therapy* and it goes like this, if you said to me, 'I'll never manage to remember all the language patterns', I could reply, 'You're right, it's obviously too complex for you to understand, you just aimed too high, give up now and let someone more intelligent have the book, you could never learn this in a million years!' Essentially, with humour, you *enter the other person's map of the world and make it absurd* by exaggerating it, you will then find the person will defend the opposite point of view!

You can have a lot of fun with this, make sure you have rapport and are respectful of the person, while being scornful of the limiting or destructive belief, they are more than their beliefs, just as you are. Also listen out for implied universals ...

'Politicians are liars', 'All women are bad drivers',
'You never let me finish my sentence',
'You always find John behind any trouble' 'Christians always let you down', 'All generalisations are lies!'

The third cluster of distinctions in the meta-model are those which straighten out *distortions,* and 'un-simplify' oversimplifications. We will deal thoroughly with the next two categories in the chapter 'Christian Life Reframing.'

Level eight

When we make two statements as if they were equal to each other in meaning we have used a *'complex equivalence'*. Common examples come up when a visually-oriented speaker says to an auditory listener, 'You are not looking at me, so you are not paying attention,' he equates looking with paying attention (because that is how it would be for him!). Of course, as with the others, there may be times when these are accurate and true, but many, many times they are not, and lead to an impoverished and often bewildering (for others) map of the world. Christians have many of these, 'you did not take communion this morning (or sing, raise hands, etc.) → you must be struggling (in sin, disobedient etc.). Other examples would be linking or equating an external behaviour (EB) like smiling, with an internal state (IS) like happiness or enjoyment. These have a similar structure to rules (if / then) and will be covered in depth later; they are detected by words like 'is, that means, therefore, equals' and is challenged by asking *'how does this (EB) mean that (IS)?'* ' how specifically does my not smiling mean I am not enjoying myself?'

'You didn't phone, you don't want to see me anymore',
'I forgot an appointment, I'm losing it',
'Nobody spoke to me at church, they don't want me there',
'He looks at other women, he's having an affair'

Level nine

With a similar structure, but much more easily detected (and also overused) are *'cause → effect'* statements: 'when you do X it makes me feel Y'. These sentences would make you believe that one person has the ability to make another feel an emotional state without any choice in the process at all. Seymour[8] says, 'One person does not have direct control over another persons emotional state. Thinking you can force people to experience different states of mind, or that other people can force you into different moods is very limiting, and causes a great deal of distress. Being responsible for the feelings of others is a heavy burden. You will have to take exaggerated and unnecessary care in what you say and do. With cause → effect patterns *you become either the victim or nursemaid of others.*' One of the outcomes of helping someone is to move them from feeling helpless, at the 'effect' end of life, to taking responsibility and responsible action – moving to 'cause'. There are many genuine cause → effect relationships in the world, God has made a universe with predictable laws of physics, but to indulge in responsibility diminishing, blame shifting like Adam and Eve did in Genesis 3 does not wash at all – 'the wife *You* gave me, the *serpent made* me!' I don't think so, do you? Words to look out for are 'makes, if – then, as you, because'. The meta-model challenge to practise is asking *'How does X cause Y?'* or *'How do you make yourself feel Y when X?'*. Get some practice in with these:

'I lost my temper because you didn't speak to me',
'The sunshine makes me happy',
'being with you makes me feel young again',

Level ten

Christians are no good at *'mind reading'* – there's no such thing as a happy medium! Many classic rows begin because one person assumes they know what the other is thinking, or think that the other person knows what they are thinking. This gives scope to either project our thoughts onto them, or blame them for not understanding you when you think they should! We have already discussed the need for sensory acuity and calibrating states so we don't hallucinate, the meta-model challenge to straighten out this distortion is *'How (exactly) do you know?'* test it on these samples;

> 'Sally is feeling depressed', 'you don't care',
> 'I know they didn't listen to me',
> 'He didn't agree, but he wouldn't admit it',
> 'I know you're wondering ...',   'You know that I hate that',
> 'You know how I feel ... ' 'You think I don't understand.'

Level eleven

One of the least 'visible' patterns of language that can paint us into a corner are *'presuppositions'*. Our presuppositions are those things that are the foundational beliefs we have about life, ourselves, others, God and the world, they are the context for any statement we make. As Christians we can usefully presuppose that God loves everyone and wants them to know Him. Other people however may presuppose they will fail, or are no good – this will seldom come out explicitly, but you will catch glimpses of a persons beliefs lurking behind *'why'* questions, e.g. 'why don't you ever do what I ask?' presupposes that you never do what I ask, 'why can't I give up smoking' assumes failure. Other words to listen out for are 'since, when, if'. There are some fun ways to use more 'surface' presuppositions, to give an 'illusion of choice', e.g. 'do you want to make these positive changes straightaway, or will you wait until this afternoon', it seems as though there is a choice, but what remains constant is the presupposition of positive change. The meta-model challenge is *'what leads you to believe that ...?'* (fill in the presupposition), gain *even more* skill with these examples (did you spot a comparative presupposition there?):

> 'When you do what I want, then I will be happy' (you are not doing what I want, I am not happy!),   'Why don't you start trying?',   'You are as lazy as your sister',
>   'Why can't I X?', 'Why can't you listen to me properly?'

Our actions, thoughts and quality of life are determined by how accurate our 'map' really is, how close to reality, how updated by the eternally true Word of God, and our map consists of the sights, sounds and feelings we re-present to ourselves and then label using words. Two of the most useful questions to focus on with your own internal self-talk to help you know what's in the map, and what's outside it? *Are 'what prevents you, and what would happen if you did?'* As we enter other people's models of the world we do so respectfully, knowing that it has been formed through their own life's experiences and the meanings they have drawn from those experiences, and our goal is to update and make more accurate their maps to Bible truth. There is a field of research called decision theory, which simply makes a distinction between what is fixed in the environment (the number of hours in a day, that we need to eat, breathe, sleep, etc.) and those things which are changeable, what is 'up for grabs'. Many times when helping individuals we find that they hold certain beliefs that they consider as fixed environmental constraints, but which are, in reality, their projection of their own beliefs and limitations onto the world. A belief is a nominalisation—you can't put it into a wheelbarrow—and what is a great service to people is finding out what they are believing and how they are believing it, in order to help them to change or update their believing so they come to more Biblical and empowering beliefs. Also when you have mastered the art of challenging oversimplified complex equivalences and cause → effects, you will understand how to break up the death-inducing legalisms, and 'bartering' prayer formulas that underestimate the wisdom and flexibility of God, and make way for a freshness and open-eyed wonder in the liveliness and dynamism of a relationship with God.

> [A word of caution – in your enthusiasm in using this powerful knowledge you could 'meta-model' some of your relationships to death! We could march around like grand inquisitors demanding 'who specifically!' and lose all our friends ... always keep in mind a) your outcome for asking for information, b) the relevance and usefulness of the information and c) that constant questioning can appear hostile and unfriendly. These questions are a great tool to apply to your own self talk, to your prayer life ('Bless John' – how specifically do I want You to bless John?') and is also a helpful tool in Bible study, to get a degree of precision in the observation, and understanding of passages.]

Hands on

- Start really listening to the conversations around you, in order of importance listen for distortions first (complex equivalences, cause → effects, mind-reading and presuppositions), then generalisations (universal quantifiers and modal operators), and lastly deletions (nominalisations first, then unspecified verbs and nouns).

Chapter 9

Patterns for Renewing your Mind.

We get more of what we focus on

Do you know anyone who worries? Anyone whose life is spoilt by unsettling discontentment? Let's face it, most people we encounter (maybe even us too) find that their thoughts seem to have 'a mind of their own', and that it isn't easy to 'take every thought captive to the obedience of Christ' (2 Cor 10.3-5). Tempting or upsetting thoughts appear to have a life of their own and come to distract and confuse us at the very worst times. Interestingly our minds will give us more of what we focus on, which is why we need to have good stuff to put in. Try this experiment; don't think of your front door — what happened? Many people think of their front door with a line through it, or some other representation of NOT-THEIR-FRONT-DOOR!

Our minds do not handle *negation*, or not-a-something. Many times, in trying to not think about a situation, we remind ourselves to represent it to ourselves so we can 'try to put it out of our minds' again. To make sense of a negative we have to represent to ourselves whatever it is we don't want to think about! this is part of the struggle that habitual worriers and smokers have, they try to 'not think of smoking, or to not think about how much they would like another cigarette', this is when we find temptation grows stronger by 'resisting' it in the wrong way. When we try not to think of a certain temptation, we are actually still giving it 'airtime' on our brainwaves, and to not think about it, we have to represent it to ourselves, and then our emotions, lusts and associations click in and seem to override our logical thinking. What is the answer? Paul in Philippians 4 gives the secret to living worry free – presenting our requests to God in prayer, with thanksgiving (vs 4-6), he also says he has learnt the secret of contentment irrespective of his circumstances – that God, and what He chooses to provide is all He needs (vs 11-13) but the jam in the sandwich is that he has learned to control his mental focus, *'Finally, brothers, whatever is true, whatever is noble, whatever is right, whatever is pure, whatever is lovely, whatever is admirable if anything is excellent or praiseworthy think about such things.'*

The story is told of a teenage girl who wanted to go to the cinema with her friends and see a film which had graphic violence, nudity and a dubious message. Her Mother had already said a decisive 'no', and so the girl follows her into the kitchen where she preparing salad for lunch. As her mother chops the ends off the carrots, peels them and places the waste on a chopping board, the girls keeps pleading 'Go on, Mum, please, everybody is going to see it, why can't I? Go on Mum, etc.' Mother cleans off the brown and floppy leaves off the lettuce, puts them on the chopping board with the other waste, then the dry and cracked onion skins, and so on, while the daughter continues her pleading and nagging, 'Why not, Mum, Oh, go on, etc.' Finally the mother takes up the chopping board with all the waste and starts to scrape it down into the bowl which contained the clean, washed salad, saying, 'Oh, all right dear.' 'Mum! what are you doing, putting all that dirty stuff in the salad bowl, stop it,' the girl shouts as she sees her meal being spoiled, 'Oh, I'm sorry,' replies the mother, 'I was just going to do with your body what you wanted to do with your mind!' – needless to say, the girl got the point and didn't go to the film. Success in bringing every thought captive comes not from being expert in what not to think about but, rather paying full attention to all the many good and true things that we can think about. Romans 16.19-20. *'Everyone has heard about your obedience, so I am full of joy over you; but I want you to be wise about what is good, and innocent about what is evil. The God of peace will soon crush Satan under your feet. The grace of our Lord Jesus be with you.'* One of the reasons that God gave us the Bible is so we would have something to dig into, investigate and apply, so that our lives really would be transformed by the renewing of the mind (Rom 12.2) What we think about is very important, before we look at some effective ways of directing our (and others) thinking, let's assimilate one more skill …

Chunking

By now this is not new to you, both the metaprogrammes of global or specific chunk size and the 'Logical levels of personality' demonstrate the usefulness of chunking. When we use the meta-model questions for specificity we are 'chunking down' we want more detail, when we 'chunk up' we move to higher levels of generalisation or abstraction. When we are negotiating or handling a meeting, we will find these skills invaluable; imagine a planning meeting where someone proposes a 'Wednesday night meeting to intercede for struggling marriages.' This is quite a detailed proposition, and as such will probably get picked on at this level of chunk size, or even lower ('I can't make Wednesdays until 8 p.m.', etc.) and we get lost in nit-picking. If there is any dissension, then 'chunk up' to 'well we all want to pray don't we?', then 'what other ways can we also help struggling marriages?', etc. When we chunk up, we find the common ground that gets obscured when we discuss things at too low a 'logical level'. Learn to play 'snakes and ladders' with words, chunking down, when someone is trying to bamboozle you with lofty abstractions, but no real content, and chunking up to find common ground, when people can't see the house for the doorknobs.

We have already started to explore the *power of questions* to direct our consciousness, now let's use this knowledge to arm us with life changing tools …

One of the things I encountered as a young Christian was the positive confession movement, where you are encouraged to find a verse from the Bible and 'name it and claim it, or confess it and possess it', while I have more than a few differences with this whole approach, I used to think 'at least they're trying to be positive', the flip side of this unfortunately is a denial of reality – too many people have become seriously ill and even died by 'claiming healing and denying the symptoms'! Anthony Robbins humorously talks about standing in his back garden and positively affirming 'there are no weeds, there are no weeds' of course, the weeds will take your garden! A more useful and honest approach is to see the weeds, pull them up and plant something beautiful in their place so there is no room for them to return. Have you ever tried any affirmations? The kind of thing where you are meant to stand in front of a mirror, maybe smile a big smile, and repeat, 'I'm happy, I'm happy, I'm happy' – of course our brain says 'No you're not!' (cognitive dissonance again, remember?) Just saying words doesn't make things true, or real, otherwise we would be living in a very different world to we are now, and my son would have a new skateboard! What our brain needs is a reason, sure we can feel happy by thinking about things in the past, but what about now? Do you think you could look at the world and get depressed? Feel that things are accelerating towards greater and greater destruction and misery and that people are all bad and want to hurt you? You bet! Just read the newspapers and watch the news, but could you also look at the world, see the revivals taking place in so many countries, the advances in medical science that are removing diseases that used to be killers, see some of the initiatives for peace and justice and feel that the world is a great place to be alive in, and that God is accelerating His work in our lifetimes? Yes, you can do that too, they are both true, but which will help you to get involved and make your life count, will enable you to live with joy and hope? The second one, probably: we can choose how we feel and how we respond to our circumstances, we can either see God and glorify Him or see the Devil and focus on him, an important principle in Romans 16.19-20 is, 'Be wise in what is good, and simple concerning evil. And the God of peace will crush Satan under your feet shortly.' When we focus on all the bad things and how the Devil seems to have the world under his sway, we feel as though we are under the Devil's feet; if, however, we are simple concerning those things and wise concerning all the things that God is doing, has done and has promised to do, we find that God gives us peace and victory over the Devil.

Here are some questions you could ask yourself in the morning as you shower or shave or dress, that will get your brain and emotions moving in the right directions, for the next ten days ask yourself these (remember to answer them fully) and notice how they destroy your ability to stay with the 'early morning cruds':

What am I happy about at the moment? (or what could I be happy about if I wanted to be?) what about that makes me happy? How does that make me feel? (feel it)

What am I grateful for in my life right now? What about that makes me grateful? How does that make me feel?

What am I excited about in my life right now? What about that makes me feel excited? How does that make me feel?

What am I proud of in my life right now? What about that makes me proud? how does that make me feel?

What am I confident about in my life right now? What about that makes me feel confident? How does that make me feel?

What am I enjoying most in my life right now? What about that do I enjoy? How does that make me feel?

What am I committed to in my life right now? What about that makes me feel committed? How does that make me feel?

Who do I love? Who loves me? What about them makes me loving? How does that make me feel?

In the evening, why not ask yourself these questions as they will reinforce in you the things that you have noticed and also what you want to continue to notice in the future:

What have I given today? In what ways have I served God?

What did I learn today?

How has today added to the quality of my life and others lives?

We're just warming to the uses of questions, because they are so powerful in directing our attention and consciousness, here are some we can ask ourselves while we are thinking about work or a task we want to do that will enable us to become even more successful

Did I give / am I giving my full effort? How can I give my full effort now? If I were to give my full effort right now, what would happen?

Did I learn / am I learning anything? How can I begin to learn something now? If I begin learning now, what would happen?

If I was going to learn something, what would it be? Where else would that learning be useful?

Some questions to ask when faced with a difficulty are the 'problem solving' question;

What can I learn from this?

What's great about this problem?

What's not perfect yet?

What am I willing to do to make it the way I want it?

What am I willing not to do to make it the way I want it?

How can I enjoy the process?

It mean seem a little weird to ask 'what's great about this problem?' but by the time you are finished with the next chapter you will understand how useful it is to ask this, and also how much appreciation it will bring into your life.

The structure of thought:

We already know that people represent internally using pictures, words and feelings, each of these major categories (modalities) has many attributes (submodalities), it was in Richard Bandler's study of subjective experience and an understanding of submodalities that has given the speed, elegance and permanence to many of the change techniques in NLP, and now you will start to learn them.

Submodalities (sbmds) are the smaller components of our internal experience, they are found in each sensory system, and are often described literally in a person's speech (refer to section on predicates). It is sbmds that let us know if something is real or not, if something is motivating, in the past or imagined, essentially they are 'the difference that makes the difference'. The following is a list of the most common sbmds, and then we will turn to how to use them. (When doing sbmd work with others I use a TV metaphor and tell them I have the remote handset for their TV and video, but they will take it away with them, this makes adjusting brightness, colour, speed, etc. perfectly understandable.)

visual: 'is the picture ...'

Bright / dark	movie / still frame	left / right / top / bottom / centre	colour / black and white
panoramic / framed	life-sized / smaller / larger	3-D / flat	clear / fuzzy

Are you seeing yourself in the picture (*disassociated*) or seeing what you saw at the time (*associated*)?

auditory: 'tell me about the sound ...'

Volume	rhythm: constant / fluctuating	tone: rich / tinny / smooth/ etc.
pauses	location, front or back	tempo

kinaesthetic: 'what do you feel ...'

temperature	texture	vibration
pressure	movement	weight, lightness

pain: (deserves its own category!) 'is there ...'

tingling	heat / cold	numbness	tension
pressure	duration	crescendo / intermittent	sharp / dull

This kind of precision in a persons internal experience gives us enormous power and flexibility to effect profound changes, we can find out the components of excellence and replicate them and also find the structure of limiting thought and behaviour and with seemingly small submodality shifts, completely change them.

One year at Spring Harvest a young man came to speak with me about something that had been done to him in the past, and that had both physical (but mainly) psychological pain attached, the pain was in his lower abdomen, he said, 'It's like red-hot sand, it's burning my guts up.' I went through an elicitation of the submodalities of how he represented it, and using the metaphor he offered me of red-hot sand, I had him dim the picture and make it black and white, he then said it looked like 'cold grey ash' in a fireplace, I then asked him if he could feel a breeze coming from one side yet, which would grow stronger and blow the ash away, which it did. He then was able to 'step back' from the original series of events and offer and receive forgiveness, because he no longer kept getting caught up in his own experience of the pain. This sounds like just playing with words, but when you realise that he was giving me a graphic description of his internal experience, and offering me a metaphor, then I could adjust the submodalities within his own metaphor and feed it back to him, with no resistance at all.

There are many techniques and exercises for you later in the book that will give you mastery in using *sbmds*, here I would like to draw your attention to just one key distinction: *association and dissociation*

Exercise:

Take the time to really imagine these things vividly, rather than just read through them.

Close your eyes and remember or imagine being at a fun fair, imagine you are sitting on a bench, with the warm sun shining down on you, you can hear all the music and noise of the fair, you can smell hot-dog stands and candy floss, and now look up and over to the rollercoaster as it stands high above you into the blue sky, and see the front car, as it clunks onto the chain drive which pulls it up the steep slope before it reaches the peak and rushes down – look again and see right at the front a person who looks just like you, in fact, just for the moment, look again and see it is you, over there on the roller coaster, and you can see all the expressions crossing the face of you over there, as you sit comfortably on the bench

Answer this question, as the roller coaster plunges down the first slope, how do you feel as you watch it from the bench?

Stand up, walk around, take some deep breaths and stretch

Now, back to the fairground, but this time, imagine you are in the first car of the roller coaster, you can hear the same music as before, and even smell the same smells, but as the car engages which the chain drive, you jerk backwards as you hear the clunk, now as it pulls you up the first steep slope, you feel a breeze tugging at your hair, and can hear some of the passengers behind you starting to scream, and now you are at the top and you are at the front of the roller coaster as it starts to plunge down on the rails.....

Stop, and answer this question; does this second memory or daydream feel any different to the first one? has it made any difference to your physiology – are you more tense? Adrenaline, heart rate?

[The point of this exercise is to highlight that in associated memories we tend to fully re-experience an event (or imagined event – such as worries!) and in disassociated memories you literally step out of the feelings of that time—This is one of the most important submodality distinctions]

Do you think that the quality & enjoyment of life might be different for these people?:

- Person A, fully associates into all painful memories, and disassociates from happy memories – this person will say they have never been happy, because they recode happy feelings out of happy times

- Person B, disassociates from painful memories, but happy ones too – this person seems emotionally frozen, remote and untouched by what happens around them, seems to have observer status even in their own lives.

- Person C, fully associates into happy memories, but also painful ones, this person is much like a child, who is on an emotional roller coaster, and who can only see their own point of view and how events make them feel.

- Person D, fully associates into happy memories and disassociates from painful ones, this means they fully enjoy the life they have had, and turn down the intensity of the bad times so they can look at what happened and learn from it without feeling dreadful over and over again.

You can teach your brain this process, where it learns to generalise the coding pattern, so that you have happy 'winning' experiences and fully feel them and the pain from the others can be disassociated from, and then what really happened can be the basis for learnings and wisdom in life.

It is important to make special note about not changing the content of memories. We cannot and will not lie and say a thing has not happened, that is moving away from what is real and true. All change that is lasting has to bring us closer to reality, that includes learning from the past and then disconnecting out-of-date feelings, so that we can respond appropriately to what is happening in our experience now.

[I presented this next segment in a 'lifers' prison, and the impact was incredible; I talked about it in terms of *memory management*]

'I would like you to take an unpleasant memory and then watch it happening to you over there, you are watching it happen on a screen, you are not seeing it happen through your own eyes, but it is like someone else took a video of it happening and is showing it to you, this is called disassociation, and it is one of the things the human brain does naturally with unpleasant experiences, like just before death your life flashing before your eyes, or in an accident, you feel strangely remote and disengaged, especially if there is significant pain, and don't we sometimes say that when someone is really distraught that they are 'besides themselves?' our language tells us a lot doesn't it? But the same can work for our pleasant memories, have you ever seen someone relive a memory? Like they are fully there? Do it now, pleasant memory, get it back, step inside, do you recover those feelings? OK so we can use this to dissociate from painful memories, but still keep our learnings, and associate into pleasant memories so we have a rich treasury of good times. NB: this helps you to deal with problems, have you ever noticed that someone else's problems are 'No big deal' and are easy to solve? you can do this with your own without being confused by your own feelings.'

One question I had when I first started doing submodality work with people was 'What if they change back again?' My experience has been that unless there are secondary gain issues, then because the changes are structural and therefore go back to being out of a persons conscious attention, they stick. It would be like not wanting to shut a book because you think the letters or words may jumble themselves up once you are not paying attention to them. Or if you use a computer, thinking that a saved file will change its name, shape and attributes when you turn the machine off! If sbmd change is not working, you will know straightaway, that is one reason you will want to test your work thoroughly *before the person leaves*. If sbmd changes do not 'stick' then it means that some part of them has a positive intention tied up in keeping the old feelings, at this point talk them through a six- step reframe, or parts alignment, to keep the positive intention and then the sbmd changes will be permanent. Chpater 11, 'A Pattern for Engagement', will address this even more fully.

A word about space and time

When a person talks to you, they are trying to share with you their internal map, they do this with words, and you will find many clues described in a person's language (for example, 'I need to get some distance, this problem is getting on top of me, etc') , also you will notice how a person maps out their thoughts with their gestures (so the person may move their hands in a pushing or pulling gesture as if to mime having problems 'in their face'). If we will pay attention to this *'mental mapping'* we will see *where* they put various thoughts in the space around them, you will know the location sbmds of a picture by where they look or move their hands, this is very useable information, because we can 'grab' a persons picture with our hands, and 'move it' (like when you mime) and if we do it right we can change the whole impact of it by moving it to a different location. For example, if a person's limiting beliefs are down and to the right (as in 'I'm downright sure of this) and their uncertainties are up and in the middle (as in 'I'm up in the air about this'), once you have discovered the locations of their limiting belief and a Biblical alternative, you may want to mime or act out moving the old false, limiting belief over to the 'doubt' location (i.e. pretend to grab it from 'downright' and move it to 'up in the air'), and bring the new Biblical belief (probably found in the uncertain position) into the location for strong convictions (pull it to the location where it's downright obvious!). It sounds simple, and it is, when it is done skilfully and ecologically, it can bring immediate and lasting psychological 'breathing space'. What we need to do is find the 'driver' submodalities (those which when we change them affect the others too) and make sure we are thorough in our elicitation and calibration of states.

The other main area that needs describing here is 'timelines', these are the submodality distinctions that help us code time, how we know something is in the past, or yet to come, how long in the past, etc. You already know the two main orientations to time; 'in time' (experiencing to from an associated perspective) or 'through time' (disassociated). Notice this now, when a person talks about the past, do they look or gesture in a certain direction? is it to the left, the right, the front, or off at an angle? Now notice with respect to the future, also with the present moment. If you were to connect up those directions for past, present and future with a line, that would be the persons 'timeline' knowing this gives you information you can immediately use to enhance rapport, but also there are many powerful timeline techniques that can remove negative influences from the past, and also create a more compelling future, you will learn these in the skills toolbox section.

Hands on

This chapter has had you doing exercises as you went along, but take the time to fully experience these activities too;

- Using the submodality list, sit down and do a thorough elicitation of submodality differences between the following states, a word of advice: you must access the state as fully as possible to get quality information.

1) Find out the differences in your internal representations of when you are motivated, and when you are unmotivated.

2) Do the same elicitation for a time when you were doubting your ability, and a time when you were unstoppable.

3) Now do it for when you were in love, and another time when you were not in love.

- For the sake of experimenting, take the representation of the thing you doubted your ability over, and adjust the submodalities to those of 'unstoppable' – it has the same 'content' but notice what has happened to your feelings about it!

- Now take a pleasant memory and go through the list of submodalities and adjust them individually, for example, turn the brightness up – does it affect the intensity of the feelings? Try turning it down, now what has happened? Do the same with locations, movement and still-frames, colours, etc., after each one, put it back how it was, but take note which submodalities are the most influential for you, do the same with the sounds. At the end of this you will know your submodality drivers (the most powerful for you will be in your preferred representational system), and how to intensify or diminish the impact of an internal representation. (As a generalisation, I have found that making an image brighter, closer, and richening up the colours intensifies, as does adding a tonal richness and resonance, rhythm and 'surround sound', alternatively, many people find intensity reduces when a picture becomes still, black and white, distant and small, and the sounds become quiet, tinny and distant).

- Take a moment to elicit your timeline, think of something that you do routinely every day, say clean your teeth, shave or drive to work. Think of doing that today, and notice the location of that picture, now think of doing it a fortnight ago, notice the location, now think of it a year ago, notice the location. Now think of doing it a week from today, again notice the location or direction that came from, same again for six months time. Simply with your finger, point towards the direction or location of the past, to the present, and to the future, as you move your finger in a line between those points, that is your 'timeline'. If you have tried to do this visually and been unsuccessful, try just 'getting a sense' of where the past and future are, you may even want to recruit a friend to watch your minimal cues for you – it will be obvious to them! Having done that, whether you are an 'in time' or 'through time' person, in your minds eye, just float up away from your timeline, and look down at it over there (if you don't like heights, just move across away from it, it's the distance you want), and just spend a few moments looking at the present, over there, then back along the past, and even the other way along your future timeline, get used to the sense of where it is, and then just 'float back' again and open your eyes.

Although you have not experienced your future yet, you do have a future timeline, because that is what you use to plan what you will do tomorrow, where you will go on holiday ,etc., it is simply the submodality location that lets you know about something that isn't in your past and isn't in your present. Also as Christians we know we have a future timeline that 'gets brighter'

→ Proverbs 4.18 *'But the path of the just is as the shining light, that shineth more and more unto the perfect day.'* But that's another story that shall be told at another time.

Chapter 10

Christian Life Reframing

I am of the opinion that Christians should be the best 'reframers' in life. What I mean by this is not that we should be 'Pollyanna' about problems, but that our positive expectation of God's involvement and positive intention will enable us to perceive empowering meanings. The context for any event sets the meaning of it. An example: you hear footsteps creeping on the landing outside your bedroom in the middle of the night, they are coming closer and then you see the silhouette of a person in the doorway moving closer, and closer … what do you feel? Fear? It all depends on the frame – if you have a toddler who is teething that will produce a different response to a burglar, or a loved one returning from a long journey, or at least I hope so! Roger Ailes[9] tells a great reframe story of when he was helping Ronald Reagan in his electioneering. His main opponent, Walter Mondale, was making Reagan's age an issue, saying he was past it, and not fit to run the country; during a stand-up debate Mondale started to bring up the age issue. Reagan's reply blew him out of the water when he turned and in his own charming style said '… and I want you to know that I will not make age an issue of this campaign. I am not going to exploit for political purposes my opponent's youth and inexperience.' Ailes simply says 'the debate was over'. Reframing is the art of 'turning the tables', of asking *'what else could this mean?'* Age could mean weakness and senility, or it could mean wisdom and experience – who decides? Many things in life do not have fixed meaning, they mean just what we decide they will, how we decide to interpret them. How can being burned at the stake or thrown to lions mean anything but terrible pain and fear and defeat? Ask a martyr – to them it means being counted worthy to suffer for the gospel, to stand for what is true and bear testimony to the greater power of God. The study of neuro-semantics is the relationship of meaning, words, state and physiology, reframing is a key vehicle in the transformation of meaning. If you read the incident with Jesus and the woman with the alabaster jar, see how Jesus changes the frame from 'wastefulness' to 'anointing His body', something that will be remembered throughout time (Matt 26.8-12), Also, His whole 'First shall be last, and least shall be greatest' completely reverses the meaning and current thinking of His disciples when it comes to ambition and servanthood (Mark 10.43-44).

You remember the presupposition about usefulness of behaviour? Reframing takes this for granted, that there is a positive intention behind every action, and also that, if we were to view every action as a skill, there will be some context where it is appropriate and useful (just not the one it's in now!), and finally, that unless predetermined by God, the meaning of an event is not necessarily fixed. My favourite example of reframing was when Leslie Cameron Bandler had a lady come to her who was a 'clean freak': she was obsessed with her carpet, and would nag at her family constantly for walking on it – not just getting it dirty, but even leaving dents in the pile! Leslie said 'I want you to close your eyes and see your carpet, and see that there is not a single footprint on it anywhere. It's clean and fluffy – not a mark anywhere,' (by this time the woman is smiling and feeling good) then Leslie continued, 'And realise fully that that means you are totally alone, and that the people that you love and care for are nowhere around.' The woman's whole face and body lurched, and she felt awful, then Leslie finished with, 'Now, put a few footprints there, and as you look at those footprints, know that the people you care about most in the world are nearby.' Here Leslie *swapped the price-tags* on a visual anchor, the woman used to see the footprints and feel bad, now she would see them and feel good, she used to see the spotless carpet and feel good, but now the meaning had been completely changed, isn't that great? Many of the Proverbs in the Bible are reframes, so are many clichés we have in our culture. I heard a spontaneous reframe on a parenting course I was running: a parent was complaining about a talkative child, who was full of a million questions, one of the other parents just said, 'Oh, he must be very intelligent', at which point the now proud mother felt like bragging about what had formerly been a 'problem'. One other example is that of a father who came to complain about his rebellious and uncommunicative teenage daughter, 'She just freezes me out, it makes me feel like a fool when I try to speak to her' (notice the cause → effect there?), to reframe it I said, 'Oh, isn't that great?, at some point her friends will want to go to a night-club, and you know there are always some older men who are out to prey on girls like your daughter – aren't you glad she knows how to freeze them out and make them feel like fools?' – it turned the 'problem behaviour' into a virtue-saving skill, then all we needed to do was to do something else with her father (which was easier now he wasn't so uptight and blaming).

In his book *Prison to Praise*, Merlin Caruthers applies one major reframe to all problems, that we can 'give thanks in everything' (1 Thess 5.18) because God 'works all things together for the good of those who love God and are called according to His purpose' (Rom 8.28). He gives an example of a man who is about to lose his job, his wife, etc., Carothers says, 'Let's thank God that you are losing your job, your wife etc., because He has used them to bring you to this place where you are trusting Him as your Saviour.' Bill Bright similarly says that a key to walking in the Spirit, is to walk by faith, and that if Rom 8.28 is true, then a sign of our trust is that we will thank God, he says, 'You can relax. You can say "thank you" when the whole world is crumbling around you because your God is sovereign and omnipotent. He holds the world in His hands, and you can trust Him. He loves you, and He promises to fight for you.' This may not seem a very sensible, realistic or easy thing to do, but the Bible gives some amazing examples, that were written for our instruction. Joseph was sold into slavery, was then falsely accused of tampering with his masters wife and thrown into prison, over time God reversed his circumstances and as he looks back on his he says 'You meant it for bad, God meant it for good' (Gen 50.20). Often time gives us a different frame, and the meaning of an event changes, so what did it mean in the first place? Richard Bandler says, 'If one day you'll look back on this and laugh, why wait?'

I was listening to a tape recently and the speaker was talking about how we preset our thinking, and then interpret events to fit what we expect. He then went on to say that if paranoia is the condition where you think that others are conspiring against you, to do you harm, then as Christians we should have the mindset of *'pro-noia'* that other people and all circumstances are conspiring to do us good. Of course, because it is a conspiracy some people will be doing us good, and serving our highest purpose in a way that seems hostile and may even look as if they are trying to harm us, but the secret is that it will work for our good ultimately, even if we don't see how yet. The basis for 'pro-noia', if you think about it, includes Romans 8.28, and a whole lot more besides. Firstly, ***God's sovereignty*** backs up and gives weight to His promise that He will work all things to our good, if you remember 'the secret' that Paul teaches about contentment in Phil 4.10-13 ('I am content when I recognise that God, and what He chooses to provide for me at this moment is all I need'), then we can learn the mirror image of the secret from Job's experience. Job, as you know, lost everything (apart from his wife – they were one flesh) and behind the scenes we are privy to Satan's attacks on him, also on the restrictions that God places on Satan's attacks, what we can therefore say is that, 'I am content (and secure) that whatever God allows to happen to me, will be for my ultimate good, and His ultimate glory.'

The second part in our foundation for pro-noia is understanding ***God's time frame***. We already have studied the fact that God is eternal, and that He knows the end from the beginning, if He says that all things will work together for our good, we can trust Him, because He can see our future now! Many times we have experienced 'failure' because we were working from too short a time frame – failure is only possible when the thing is finished, and with God that needn't be when we thinks it's over. Abraham could have felt a failure, he was a hundred years old, and Sarah's womb was dead, when a thing is too late, when it is over, then we can feel we have failed – but even then God has the last word. If you view the cross as the disciples did, then it was a failure, God's Messiah was arrested and brutally murdered, it was the end, and they felt bitter disappointment – but with hindsight, a different time-frame, we can see the cross as the turning point in human history, and the greatest victory for us; what changes failure into victory? The ability to step out of our limited human timeframe, and into God's unlimited timeframe. When we look back from Heaven, from the successful completion of our lives, from the position of being face to face with God, with no more tears, sorrow or pain, we know it will all make sense, we will be able to look back and see how it all worked for our good – if that is the case, then let's trust God now, shall we?

Another factor in developing Biblical pro-noia is that the Bible is full of *God's promises*, not only do we have countless examples of God's working circumstances to the good (Daniel in the furnace or the lions den did not seem good at the time, but as the story unfolds, we understand them differently) but also many promises to His people, and to us. We don't have to guess what God's will is, He has revealed it in His Word, and His Word is full of marvellous promises to us (2 Pet 1.3-5). One of the central promises to us, that gives us the ability to take life in our stride is that *God is Redeemer*, that He has the ability, and desire, to 'turn the tables', to bring good out of evil and suffering. God has not promised us an easy life, He has promised that we will grow in the 'family likeness', and that after we have been through these 'light and momentary afflictions' we will hardly consider them comparable to 'the exceeding weight of glory' to be revealed in us (2 Cor 4.16). Having set a context for reframing, let's spend some time learning how we can transform meaning for ourselves and for others

New directions for Christian thinking

I have a friend who is a Christian conjuror, and I have sat just inches away from him watching him do 'sleight of hand' where an object appears, disappears or changes into something else, and I can't for the life of me see how he does it. These following language patterns have been called 'sleight of mouth' because the listener can give you something in terms of words or meanings, and 'as if by magic' old untrue and disempowering meanings can disappear or be transformed into something else.

You remember *cause → effect* and *complex equivalences* from the chapter on language? These patterns will work most elegantly when you have a 'problem' presented to you as 'External Behaviour (EB) *causes* Internal State (IS)' or 'External Behaviour (EB) *equals or means* Internal State (IS)' we will have many examples, so keep reading and you will master this. Hall and Bodenhamer talk about a 'magic meaning box', the formula inside the box is 'This EB "is", equals or causes this IS', and then give five questions to elicit the cause → effect (C→E) and complex equivalence's (CEq) from any statement.

- How does this comprise a problem for you? (C→E)
- What makes it so? (C→E)
- How does this comprise a problem for you? (C→E)
- What does this mean to you? (CEq)
- What meaning do you give to this? (CEq)

As you listen to the responses you will hear Causation beliefs marked by words like (*because, if, when, then, so that* etc.) and meaning beliefs (CEqs) marked out by (*is, means, equal,* etc.). When you have got a 'this means that' or 'this causes that' statement, you are ready to work a little 'magic'.

Not all of them work equally well all the time, but as you grow in your ability to use them, you will find more and more which patterns to use when. Let's have a couple of examples to run through each of these patterns:

'You being late (EB) means you don't care (IS)' and 'You saying that (EB) makes me mad (IS)' or 'Whenever I am tempted, it upsets me. It makes me feel such a sinner, and a failure, I hate not keeping my rules for that purpose' This last one would be 'not keep my rules or standards (EB) = feel like (or am) a sinner & failure (IS)'

If you are going to operate from their presuppositions and map of the world you could think of staying *'in the box',* here you have four choices, each of them go 'it doesn't mean this, it means that':

1) **Redefine EB,** 'how recently have you checked that your rules are accurate, who are your rules according to? You? God? Other people in your church? Is it against your rules to be tempted or give in to temptation? Or *redefine IS*, I would have thought the real sin and failure would be when someone gives up and stops learning, in this life we won't be perfect but we can keep learning, it would be more wrong to ignore God's offer of forgiveness and a fresh start, wouldn't it?

2) **Apply to self / other / listener**: 'does that mean when you're late you want people to know you don't care?', 'If Jesus wasn't late in coming back by some peoples standards, we probably would never have known Him', 'Does that mean if I don't live up to your rules I am a failure too?', 'Does that mean if you don't live up to my rules you are even more of a failure?' 'Does that mean that Jesus was a sinner and a failure—it says that He was tempted in every way like we are? (Heb 4.15) 'Would you believe me if I said this?', Does this hold true for your mother / Father / Pastor / best friend / worst enemy?'

3) **Counter example:** have you ever been on time but not cared? Have you ever been late but cared deeply? Has there ever been a time when you were not tempted? When you didn't give in to it? When you easily kept your own rules? (this is great when someone makes an identity level statement, 'I am.....)

4) **Reverse presupposition:** now that you think about it again, how could my being late actually mean I care about you? How could your increasing awareness of temptation actually mean you were growing in holiness?

> [Now we step *out of the box* and explore the impact that other frames will have on the meaning. First we will 'pre-frame', i.e. go to a time *before the box* — this is particularly easy having said all we have about God!]

5) **Assuming a positive prior intention:** 'I understand you upset yourself because I was late, it really is important to you to know I care, isn't it?', 'Living up to your standards must be really important to you, I guess you must be really pressing on to know God more. And since you want that, perhaps a different attitude towards failure will help you stay in touch with God more', 'What good things do you think God has in mind for you to get from this? If God was

trying to teach you just one thing from this, what would it be?

6) **Assuming positive prior causation:** 'It seems important to you to be holy, so you have probably taken on some limiting rules because you had some disappointing experiences and wanted to protect yourself from more pain. I wonder what other beliefs and principles you could live by that would enable you to enjoy a free and full life, like Jesus offers? Hall has one that goes, 'Sorry that I'm late, because I looked forward to this meeting all week and have really wanted to meet with you. Repeated throughout the day I have thought about the possibilities we have together. So I do apologise for getting here late. I should have considered the traffic at this hour and the possibility of an accident – which of course happened. Guess I was thinking more of you than those details' – who could stay mad at that? This brings up an important point in conversational reframing, we *do not use it to wriggle out of our responsibilities* – if we are late, or wrong, we should apologise, and put it right.

> [Now we move to the other end of time, we can 'post-frame' with hindsight, moving *after the box:*]

7) **A good place to start is the first outcome:** 'What results do you get from believing I don't care about you if I'm late?' How do you feel when you label yourself failure and sinner, does this give access to useful resources and states?

8) When we stack these results we get a *consequential outcome:* 'Imagine believing this and experiencing those results for the next five to ten years, what comes out of that? Is that good? What other results would probably result too?'

9) A favourite of mine is *eternity framing:* 'In the light of eternity, how much do you think it will matter that I was half an hour late? As you look back, was it worth trying to make me feel bad? If you were to see things from God's perspective, with all the other things going on both good and bad in the world, how much do you think it matters? When you look back from Heaven, how will you feel about holding a belief that limited your actions and choices so much?

10) Another direction we can take our questioning involves going 'under the box', that is to *'chunk down'*, both in specificity, how do you represent 'lateness' or 'failure' etc.?

What pictures, sounds, feelings, submodalities do you use? How do you represent the action of failing as 'making' you a failure? Also in a reality chunk down where we ask 'how do you know?' Bandler tells of a time when someone came to him and said 'I'm depressed', to which he replied, 'How do you know? You may be ecstatic and just not realise it yet!' . These are the meta-model responses to challenge mind-reading 'how do you know that my being late means I don't care?'

> [Now the fun can really begin, as we *chunk up* logical levels, we can 'out-frame' a belief or statement, by moving over the box:]

11) The first and most obvious chunk up is to *abstract EB or IS*: there seems to be a relationship between time and caring, so 'If I showed up even later, would that mean I cared about you less? What about if I arrived a few minutes early, would that mean I care about you more?'

12) *Model of the world:* again you will see meta-model thinking in this, we recognise that a person is speaking only from their map, and quite possibly eternal truth, so we can ask 'according to whom? or says who?', this gives us the freedom to reduce its intensity to more realistic proportions 'So, it seems to you, at the moment ...' ask yourself 'who made that map, and are they worth modelling in this area of life?' Did they know all there is to know about this? Did they get the results that I would like? This is particularly useful when we get stuck on a persons rules and laws of conduct, which may well be a chunk down of a Biblical principle. Everything we ever say and think is dated and based on what we know at the time, only God's word is otherwise.

13) If we move a step further than just applying the statement to ourselves or another, we can do some *allness framing* – this means applying the statement to everyone, including Jesus, this usually breaks up, or loosens up the limitations of the thinking. 'So, what would happen if everyone in the whole world held this belief, would that be good?, what would be the consequences, are there any exceptions? Notice these reflect some of the well-formed outcome questions, particularly if you force into a *'have-to'* frame, where all people must, all the time!

14) *Identity framing* applies the statement at a very high logical level, 'so how I handle time determines whether I am a caring or an uncaring person? is everyone who is ever late uncaring?,

15) Another well-formed question would bring in *ecology framing:* 'is it good for you and others to have these attitudes towards failure and success, both in the short and long-term? does these beliefs enable you to move in the directions you would like to go?

As you practise these you will come to have some that suit your way of thinking best, that's great, so make sure you master the use of the others too, for the sake of the people you will be helping in finding new, Biblical beliefs. (I strongly recommend 'Mindlines' by Hall & Bodenhamer.)

Action signals

Few people will thank you for finding alternative meanings for things they are happy with, it is usually only 'problems' that need reframing (of course, you may well see something that they cannot – the only thing we cannot see is our own blind spots). As a leader or counsellor, consider how people often get stuck on the negative emotion and don't go beyond it – here we can help them get unstuck again. Just imagine for a moment that *God has a positive intention* for allowing us to be able to feel these emotions, what would they mean then? If God wanted them to be useful for us, what would their message be? Use these questions as a larger (and Biblically true) 'frame' to put round the feelings and notice how your client begins to think in new ways.

A negative feeling or emotion happens for a reason, and if we assume a positive intention, then we would do well to find it out. Sometimes when we feel something negative, it may not be 'real' and is therefore due to our wrong *perception*, in which case when we become aware of that, we can change it. Alternatively, it may be giving us a message that we are going about things in a way that is not working, in which case we need to change our *procedure*: let's go through the list of 'negative' emotions, and find out how much they are really our 'friends', Tony Robbins says they are a 'call to action'.

- *discomfort or pain*: we know that pain serves us, if we didn't have pain, we would never know when our body was damaged, or that something was wrong, pain or discomfort is a great motivator, its message is 'something is not right, do something else', other names for the emotions under this heading are – boredom, impatience, unease or distress.

- *fear or anxiety*: the message is 'something is going to happen that needs to be prepared for, are you ready?' I never have anxiety about speaking to hundreds of people unless I have not prepared properly, in which case I review my material and check that I have done everything else within my power to be ready, I also make the decision to have faith, to trust that God knows what He is doing in letting me be here!

- *hurt*: often the message is that we have an expectation that has not been met, especially when it involves somebody else. We may have a wrong perception, we can ask 'is there really loss here? Or am I judging this situation too soon or too harshly, is there something going on here that I don't know about? If there really is an issue, it may be appropriate to communicate our feelings with the other person, the same goes for ....

- *anger:* the message is that an important rule or value has been violated, by someone else, or maybe by you. Ask yourself, have I understood this situation correctly? did the other person know that I held this rule? Even if they did violate one of your rules, are your rules right, fair and to be universally applied? And in the long run, is it true that this person cares about me, is it important for me to share my feelings with them, can I restate my values to them in a way that prevents this happening again?

- *frustration:* is a frequently misunderstood 'action signal', the message is 'I'm sure I could be doing better than I am at the moment', we feel frustration when we know it's not over, but we just aren't getting it right yet. The solution is the '3 minute seminar', know what you want, take action, notice what you are getting and be flexible in your approach – accept all results as feedback and guidance towards success! frustration is completely different to.....

–   *disappointment:* which tells us that a goal or hope we had is probably not going to happen, it's over, we don't feel disappointment when there is a chance, we feel frustration. It may be that we have judged the whole thing too early, when we do that we cease to notice any solutions that do turn up! The solution is to take into account the new information you now have and set a new goal. Remember the lesson from Abraham's life, just because it seems too late, doesn't mean a thing when the God of the impossible is involved.

–   *guilt and conviction:* the message is 'you have violated one of your own (or God's) highest standards, you must do something immediately to make sure you don't do it again, the pain of guilt is there to help us from going and doing it again and again, and conviction is to draw us to God to own up, receive forgiveness, and the power to not do it again.

–   *inadequacy:* the message is 'you don't presently have the skills for the task at hand', some people are capable and have low self-esteem, they will need to adjust their perception to let them get on with it, others, however will need to get more understanding, information, tools and confidence. Inadequacy can help us avoid the trap of having confidence beyond our competence.

–   *feelings of overwhelm:* the message is that we are trying to give attention to too many things, we end up giving decent attention to nothing which causes it to increase! the solution is to re-evaluate what is most important to you in this situation, if necessary grab some paper and write it down, prioritise and then do only what is most important, get first things first.

–   *loneliness:* we have neglected our need for belonging, the message is 'you need to connect with someone', the solution is to identify what kind of connection you want to make, and then reach out and make it, call a friend, go to church, or whatever.

So called 'negative feelings' are actually *action signals*, they draw your attention to what needs doing, where things are not yet right, if we try to ignore them, they are like a young child wanting you to notice them, they will get louder and more disruptive the more you try to ignore them! Instead, recognise the positive message and intention they have, even be grateful for them, the sooner you listen, the sooner the message will stop. Do exercise caution in reframing – we must never think that we can diminish the impact of God's Word by subjecting it to 'spin', instead we find that we uncover more, not less, of what God is saying.

Hands on

- Listen out for statements that have the EB = IS structure, especially in your own self-talk, or ones that you have heard before and practise using the reframing patterns in this chapter.

- Write a list of all the emotions or states that you experience in your average week, set them in order, and notice how many you habitually access. Now add to the list emotions and states that you would like to experience more often – outrageousness? Ecstasy? Joy? Hilarity? Joyfulness? Peaceful calm? Determination? Optimism? Look at the lives of those you admire and work out what states and emotions they operate from, add those too.

- Think back over times when you have felt negative emotions and re-evaluate them in the light of the message they may having sending you, and also what could have happened if you had understood that way.

Chapter 11

A Pattern for Engagement

Introducing an encounter

Would you like to make positive changes in your life? Are you involved in caring for any other people? You would like to learn how to make elegant, permanent and painless changes, wouldn't you? We can learn to model some of the ways that Jesus helped people change, although they are presented in quite a different way here. This chapter presents an outline (not a formula, more like a map) that will help you to engage in changework with confidence, and will also give you a place to start looking if you get results you weren't expecting. One of my main desires in writing this book was to make transferable the skills and perspectives needed to do effective Christian changework, my hope is that once you have a degree of competence, you will press on to mastery by continual use – reach out and help people!

Before you meet with a person who is coming for help, take the time to remember the values we operate from, also the presuppositions (see earlier chapters), take time to pray and 'breathe spiritually'. A word to the wise, 'the Jericho road sets its own agenda'. Sometimes we find needs as we go through life, and we are able to be good neighbours – we need also to recognise that Jesus was centred and focused, He never went 'hunting' for problems. The hardest lesson to learn is waiting, sometimes, because we care, we can get sucked into the perceived 'urgency' of a persons problem, this can take the form of phone calls at all hours, asking for help in making routine decisions (shifting responsibility onto you), and a sense of dependence on you – interestingly, Jesus who is love incarnate, never got drawn in this way. Lazarus was sick, and going to die, the sisters sent a message for Him to hurry, but He didn't, and it all turned out fine (John 11). They could have said that His being late meant He didn't care, but after the last chapter you know that's not true. I have learned that, unless there are definitely reasons to do otherwise, people can wait to see me. I have had phone calls in the night, that could have waited until the morning – I know I can't give my best when I am half asleep, and I will only reinforce the sense of urgency in the person. If a person is sinking in quicksand, we have the choice of jumping in with them, or staying out and throwing them a line – learn to wait. The other benefit of learning to wait is avoiding the trap of hallucinating what we think the other person is thinking, and putting our words into their mouths when they are unforthcoming (this doesn't work – I tried it!). Instead we can trust that their unconscious mind wants the issue sorted; this increases the amount of leverage (see later), highlights areas of secondary gain and bypasses resistance – learn to be quiet, become curious instead of uncomfortable.

Before we embark on our discussion of the elements of a therapeutic encounter, one global chunk way of seeing the process is *set up / upset / setdown*. Firstly, the 'set-up' is how things are perceived, the behaviours, beliefs, physiology and internal representations, and the patterns of interaction with others that constitute the 'problem' (imagine it as an arrangement of objects on a table). Then comes the 'upset', which is whatever we do to 'jog' the table, any strategic or incidental interventions that we do. By 'upset' I am not implying that it is unpleasant, only that it changes the position, configuration and relationship of the pieces. Finally there is the 'set-down' which is where the objects come to rest, this is the end result of an integration or settling process, and also becomes the setup for subsequent involvement. This process of set-up, up-set, set-down, occurs at a small level repeatedly in an encounter, and also at a high level over the period of time between appointments. The important thing is to be continually moving in the directions of choice, improvement and conformity with truth.

The Map...

The 'client' needs to feel:

1) **Rapport:** the first place to start is rapport, a person feeling they can trust you, that you are interested and will listen, that you will respect them and can help them (if these things are not true, do them a favour and send them home!). Start by matching and mirroring, listen out for 'impact words' that seem emotionally potent, they are existing word-anchors (you may want to use them to elicit responses later). Notice which representation systems they use, particularly if they use a different system to 'normal' when they describe the problem, this gives a major clue to where to intervene. Use all the rapport skills you can to 'enter their map'.

2) **Establish desired state & present state:** start by asking the 'outcome questions', find out what they want, people often know what they don't want, but that is only feeding a negation into their RAS. Use the meta-model questions to get precision answers, find out 'how will you know when you've got X?' What will they see, hear, feel, etc.? We need to have clear representations of what needs to happen, what needs to stop happening and what resources are needed to move from the present 'problem' state, to the desired state. An effective way to get this information would be to ask 'If, while you slept tonight, a miracle happened and changed this problem, but you didn't know because you were asleep – when you woke up, what would be the first thing you would notice that would let you know the miracle had happened?' Then use the precision questions to get sensory specific information, and keep asking 'what else?, what else?' (if you want to, as they access these things, you can always anchor them for use as a resource later).

A fuller way of gathering this information at a more structural level is to use the *behaviour model* to find out the patterns for present state and desired state, this assumes the 'problem' is an achievement and asks 'how do you do that?', this line of questioning, is very thorough and comprehensive, be sure you need all the information or don't ask for it:

   a)   Describe the behaviour you want to change now and describe the behaviour you are committed to experience in the future

b) Describe the emotions and feelings you want to change now and describe how you want to feel in this situation from this day forward.

c) Now identify the *patterns of belief:*
Problem state – what would I have to believe in order to feel this way? (global beliefs / identity beliefs, and any reference experiences I have used in the past to back them up), what rules would I have to have in order to have this problem? what values does this problem reflect? How have these patterns of belief met the following human needs? (grade them from 0-10) Certainty, variety, significance, connection, growth, contribution?

Desired state – what would I have to believe in order to feel the way I want to feel? To behave the way I want to behave? To produce the results I truly want? What rules would empower and enable me? What values would I need to have? At what level (0-10) will these new patterns meet my human needs? certainty, variety, significance, connection, growth, contribution?

d) Identify *patterns of language:*
Problem State – what words do I speak with tremendous emotional intensity on a consistent basis that may be limiting the quality of my life (self talk, 'incantations', intensifiers and softeners?), what disempowering questions do I ask myself, and what are the hidden presuppositions inside them? What are the 'toxic' metaphors I use to describe the problem area? How have these patterns met my human needs in the past (0-10)? certainty, variety, significance, connection, growth, contribution?

Desired state – what words could I use on a consistent basis in order to produce the emotions / behaviours I want for my life now? (self-talk, incantations, intensifiers and softeners), what questions can I consistently ask that will give me access to the resources I desire? what can I truthfully presuppose? What metaphors can I use? How much more fulfilling will these new patterns be to my human needs? (0-10) certainty, variety, significance, connection, growth, contribution?

e) Identify *patterns of physiology:*
Problem State – what do I have to do with my body in order to produce / be in this state continually? (Movement / submodalities), what about posture? breathing? Facial expressions? Gestures? Muscular tension relaxation? (Upper & lower body). What about biochemistry; breathing (enough oxygen)? hydration (enough water)? Diet / Blood sugar? Are you exercising? What is your current diet? What about body structure? Balance? Tension? These patterns have met my needs at the following level (0-10), certainty, variety, significance, connection, growth, contribution.

Desired state – How would I need to use my body in order to produce / be in this desired state consistently? posture? breath? facial expressions? gestures? muscle tension? Biochemistry; how would I need to breathe? hydration? diet / blood sugar? exercise? what would my diet need to be in order to be my absolute best? Are there any structural adjustments to make? do I need to consult a Doctor? These new patterns are more fulfilling to my human need at these levels (0-10), certainty, variety, significance, connection, growth, contribution?

> [Whichever parts of this you use, make sure you have a well-formed outcome, a clear representation of the present sate and the desired state, and that you have a Biblical and healthy alternative. Often clarifying things this much will make a solution apparent, and by the time you have completed the next stage, you may find that the changes occur spontaneously without any further intervention.]

3) *Leverage:* For change to really take place, there must be leverage, this is encapsulated in three beliefs: this MUST change (not should, or I wish), I must change it (we must not take responsibility away from people, this leaves them powerless in our absence) and I CAN change it (with God's power and our help). Of the times when changes have been hard to make, or have not been permanent, the central issue has been one of leverage – that the person is committed to change. You already understand that pleasure and pain are

the twin forces we can use to gain leverage, but first let's deal with the issue of secondary gain – it is fair to assume that there are mixed neuro-associations regarding the 'problem' otherwise the person would have just decided to change it and that would be that! If they have failed with their conscious mind, there must be an underlying, unconscious reason for the behaviour to continue, either that in some way it protects from pain or creates some kind of pleasure, to find out what specifically, ask:

a)   what are the positive benefits of not changing? What does it do for you?

b)   what would be the cost of changing? What would you lose?

c)   what are the positive benefits of changing now, what pleasure will you gain?

d)   what is the cost of not changing now? How much pain will it incur?

> [These questions simply find out if there has been the perceived comfort of procrastination etc. To deal with secondary gain, either use a six step reframe or a 'visual squash' (see toolbox section). Now to increase leverage....]

If a person is able to continue in a problem behaviour, say smoking or overeating, they are only able to do it by disassociating from the present and future consequences, if they saw that this cigarette or doughnut was costing them vitality, they would be more motivated to stop! We use pain and pleasure inducing questions to reconnect those consequences with the actions

Pain inducing: 'How much has this action / belief / attitude cost me?' What have I lost as a result of it? What haven't I done? Where haven't I gone as a result of it? What negative emotions do I consistently experience as a result of this? What has this action / belief / attitude cost me in terms of my health? Career? Finances? Social life? Family and loving relationships? Relationship with God? Self esteem?

Pleasure inducing: 'What benefits will I gain as a result of this change? What positive emotions will I feel as a result of this? What other areas of my life will improve too? What specifically will I gain in terms of my health? Career? Finances? Social life? Family and loving relationships? Relationship with God? Self esteem?

[As we ask these questions, we want more than answers, we want the person to access those answers fully, to reassociate into the pain and the pleasure, because then we have helped them build a propulsion system that moves them away from the old behaviour and towards the new, we have harnessed the power of the unconscious mind.]

An even more powerful use of these questions is the 'Dickens pattern', developed by Anthony Robbins, based on *A Christmas Carol* – you remember the story? Scrooge is an old grouch, who dislikes everyone and lives to please himself and gain financial wealth, but on Christmas eve he is visited by three spirits. The ghost of Christmas past shows him where he made decisions as a child and as a young man, and how they cost him his love, cost him warmth and companionship in his life. The ghost of Christmas present then shows him what those decisions are costing him in terms of how others view him, all the warmth he is missing out on, and what a miserable existence he is living. The crunch comes when the ghost of Christmas future shows him the emptiness, futility and bitterness of his end, how people are glad to see the last of him, it is too much for Scrooge to bear, he breaks down, crying 'enough'. Then the ghost of the future in so many words says 'These things are not yet so, they are but a shadow of the future', 'It's not too late?' asks Scrooge, and then the clock strikes and he is a changed man! We can stack the leverage high when we use time and consequences:

Past: As you look back now, see how much it has cost you, what has it cost you in your health, etc? Pain inducing questions, pause after each question and ask them to feel it, now.

Present: again repeat the pain inducing questions but what it is costing now, what they can't do, now etc. and ask them to feel it fully.

Future: this is the clincher, 'I want you to go in your mind, a year from now, if you haven't changed this now, and look back and see how much more pain it will have cost you, what has it cost you in your emotions? In your self esteem, how do you feel about yourself knowing that you're that kind of person? What has it cost you in your relationships? Who has had to leave your life because it's too much to bear? What kind of people do you associate with now? How much has it cost you financially? Spiritually? In your health? Look at yourself in the mirror, see the cost, how do you feel about that as you feel it fully now? Now take all of that pain, like a heavy sack of potatoes, and drag it to 5 years from now, if you didn't change – what do you see now as you look in the mirror? are you proud of that, how does it feel? what has not changing cost you in your emotional life? who is still around? how do your children think about you now? do you want them to model you in this area of life? what has it cost you in your relationship with God, etc? You can continue this as appropriate 10, 20 even 40 years into the future, and stack the emotions high, load it fully that they will reach a threshold of pain and change will become a 'must', just like Scrooge. You can then (if necessary) take them through a future journey of all the benefits and changes they will experience, not just now, but through time if they make the changes now, stack loads of pleasure.

You may find more 'provocative' ways of getting leverage, using humour, exaggeration (see precision & reframing chapters) also the sleight of mouth patterns may loosen up a persons tightly held views. Robbins used to tell people he had a 'one-stop therapy' reputation to uphold, and they would ruin it if they didn't change, so he would make them write a long and detailed list of all their reasons to convince him that they really must change – he would get them to produce the leverage, or he would say he would send them home!

Our culture tends to undervalue *consequences;* often if we saw what an action would result in a year from now, we wouldn't consider it. At a 'meta' level we are teaching the person to look beyond the immediate, to have a sense beyond immediate gratification, here we are putting the axe to the root of the tree which bears 'feels good, is bad for me, others, etc.' fruit. The Bible teaches this principle and does not shy away from using extreme and emotionally loaded examples – read Prov 7.6-23, an ox to the slaughter, a bird to the snare! James 1.14-16 does the same, if temptations are 'lies in disguise', we could think of them as the bait on a hook – no sensible fish (or person) is going to take a sharp, barbed, death inducing hook and put it into his mouth, so the fisherman covers the hook with a nice juicy worm – so tasty, so attractive! James simply instructs us, 'See the worm, remember the hook, see the temptation, remember the price.' In this sense the Bible takes a tempting stimulus, and instructs our brains to go in a new direction, to learn a new neuro-associaction 'see this, do this' or with temptation, 'see this (bait), think this (hook)' to 'swish' our brain in this new way, means that we can 'rewire' our neuro-associations, but more about that later.......

4) *Interrupt the 'limiting pattern'*: by now we have a good idea of what the person wants, what they don't want (and how they do it) and a good amount of leverage, the next bit can be great fun. If I am listening to a CD and a song comes on that I dislike, it doesn't mean the CD player is bad, or wrong, I just have to change what it is doing. If I decide to play a different CD I have to take the old one out first, this is equivalent to a 'pattern interrupt'. For some people, being in rapport with you, or talking about what they want or especially the leverage section will have already interrupted their pattern, so let's think more fully about why this is important...... If we thought of a limiting pattern as the opening bars of a song (a blazing row may be the 1812 overture!) there is a set order of the notes, a 'syntax', a pattern interrupt will jolt the notes or order of notes so that something else happens. Have you ever been engrossed in conversation and a person comes and asks you the time, or directions? When you have answered this interruption you say 'now, where were we?' if there are enough interruptions, we can't get the topic back at all. I remember a time when I was suffering from a terrible headache, the 'phone rang and it was vital that I pick up my children from the other side of town, my car was unavailable so I cycled, after I got the children home I realised the emergency had 'interrupted' my headache! Don't we often do this with young children, trying to distract them from their cut knee?

If we interrupt the syntax of a problem often enough we will make it harder to access. This leads to a second comment about interrupts; if behaviour is state dependent, then we want to interrupt the state that allows the behaviour to happen, for example, I work in a Prison and all of the inmates have killed someone; this is a highly specialised behaviour that requires a definite 'state' of mind and body, if it wasn't state dependent we wouldn't have prison overcrowding. While understanding the circumstances that led to the crime, etc., may be interesting, to regain that information fully, the person has to re-access the state – this does not seem like a good idea to me!

The more we access a state, the more easily we can access it in the future, for we are strengthening the neural connection (or widening the pathway across the farmers field) – often traditional, caring counselling has focused so much on a persons terrible history, that it trains the person to 'visit' painful and disempowering states more and more easily. I care deeply about the people I see, and I show that care by interrupting the state so they are able to have the psychological space to make some changes. Have you ever been in a 'stupid' state, when you could hardly spell your own name? Is this the best time to try to make decisions about your future career? Of course not! We need to get into a clear, decisive and confident state, a state where we are holding all the Biblical teaching and principles we know. Similarly it seems madness to get someone in their 'problem' state and expect them to be resourceful and cooperative. If we are 'sympathetic' we may only reinforce the problem, let's be caring and *'break the state'*.

A woman came to me who had been suffering from depression for over five years, as she walked past my office window she had her head up, breathing fully, looking around at the trees and enjoying the sunny day – she came into the coffee lounge outside my office and was looking around and 'checking out' what to expect. She came in and sat down and straightaway her head went down, her face muscles went slack and she started saying 'I just don't know what's wrong with me.....' in a slow and mopey tone of voice, I stood up and said, 'Wait! we haven't started yet!' I smiled at her and extended my hand, she stood, smiled back and said 'Oh, sorry', we then talked for another couple of minutes in an 'up' kind of way, then I shared with her how she had let me interrupt her state, and some of the ways she could use this information. Was I being shallow? flippant? I don't think so, if I fall down stairs and break my leg, will it really get better if I keep throwing myself downstairs again and again until the pain goes away? Sometimes people only need a good listening to, and a shoulder to cry on – but they are not the people who come for changework, this is the beauty and power of the Body of Christ, through the skills, love and differing temperaments of the church we can offer care, support *and change*.

So what are some of the ways we can interrupt somebody's pattern? Sometimes simply to change topic rapidly and inappropriately, to say something irrelevant, humour, surprise, etc. (there are exercises in the toolbox section). Also when we get leverage it breaks up the old feelings associated to the behaviour, a sleight of mouth reframe when it really 'hits home' can knock our brain sideways, also a thing called a 'double bind'.

Double binds are better demonstrated than described, Bandler tells of a young lady who 'couldn't say no' to her friends, and that terrible things would happen if she did ever say 'no' to anyone (they may even die), it was a group therapy setting so Bandler instructed her to go round the group and say 'no' to each member. The double bind is that she either said 'no' to them, or she would have to say 'no' to him! in this case it gave a highly emotional counter-example to her belief, and was the start of her recovery. Another kind of double bind is in the form of 'What do you do when the teacher says 'disobey me'?' Recently my youngest son was whinging at the meal table, 'Can I get down?' My wife turned, and with a big smile said, 'No, stay up the table and moan at us'. He then had the choice of stopping moaning, or it was framed as obedience, it broke his state, he looked confused, then started laughing and got on with his food. Paul Watslawick in his excellent *Language of Change* also lists ambiguous language, puns, exaggeration, the illusion of choice (would you like to sit and make those changes in this chair, or that chair? – there is choice in the chair, the changes are presupposed). Milton Erickson also would 'prescribe symptoms' – he would instruct overweight people to eat more and gain weight, those who were 'overtaken' by the urge to do something would have to do it at a fixed time whether they wanted to or not. The thinking behind this is that it firstly puts the client back at 'cause' not effect, it is something *they* do, it does not happen *to them*, secondly it changes the whole relationship of the person to the 'problem', it may become distasteful, inconvenient and loses its 'compulsive' element – changes take place at multiple levels with this approach. A caveat would be that we would not prescribe something illegal, dangerous or scripturally unecological.

Another way we can interrupt someone's pattern is by using a *metaphor* or story. Jesus did this frequently, and He would have surprise endings – He would 'pace' the listeners experience, using familiar objects and characters, and the jolt His listeners by having something unexpected happen – the good Samaritan is a good example. Metaphors give us the chance to engage our listener with something they expect to be meaningful, so they engage in a transderivational search for symbols and meanings, and then we are able to 'lead' them into a different perspective, or at least to loosen up their former limiting beliefs and attitudes. David Gordon tells a story to illustrate; imagine there is a station master who owns his own railway station, it's his pride and joy, and he loves to watch the trains, passengers and cargo moving like clockwork in his station. One day a man knocks on his office door and says, 'I'd like to bring my elephant into your station please', 'No way!' the station master erupts. 'This is a railway station, not a zoo, get out of here.' The elephant owner has three choices, he can walk away from the station saying the station master wasn't ready for elephants anyway (therapists would say he was 'resistant'), he can back his elephant up and charge it at the big doors at the front of the station (this is what many therapists try to do with 'resistant' clients!) OR he can go to the station up the track, put his elephant in a cargo carriage and take it into the station masters station that way, when it arrives he can open the doors of the carriage and ask the station master to see if he thinks it 'fits' in his station, if it does – it can stay, if it doesn't then it's time for the elephant to continue its journey. A story or metaphor 'packages' the elephant (change, or new resource or perspective) in a way that side-steps 'resistance', and gives people the chance to evaluate it from the inside, stories open up our filters. I make these asides about resistance because it has been said that 'resistance' is an indication of the inflexibility of the communicator. The other beauty of stories is that they capture our imagination, and even if we decide not to 'take on board' the message inside, 'A mind once stretched by a new idea never regains its original dimensions' as Oliver Wendell Holmes once said.

Not only can we interrupt the sequence of a problem, we can interrupt it using our knowledge of submodalities, an example might be the *scramble pattern......*

Exercise

Read through the instructions completely before doing the exercise.

a) Think of an experience with another person that has really bothered you in the past

b) Run through a movie of that experience from a disassociated point of view, maybe from the other persons elbow, or from a flies eye view, from the ceiling lampshade, etc.,

c) When you get to the end of it freeze frame and get ready for some fun..

d) Choose some utterly inappropriate music, like circus music, *the Smurfs* or *the Birdie Song,* jump into that frozen frame and run the movie backwards FAST, all sounds, movements really fast backwards like reverse on a video recorder, see the words going back into their speakers' mouths, run it through in about 2 or 3 seconds, change the colour tint over the picture say, pink, or golden and run it backwards even faster 2 more times

e) Now think again of that person / situation and notice how differently you feel now.

The purpose of this exercise is to demonstrate how quickly you can change the way you represent a previously unpleasant experience sot hat when you think of it now it makes you smile, laugh or just feel so neutral that you wonder why it bothered you in the first place. Remember, it is through your internal representations that you create whatever emotions you experience. The principles of rewind and scramble do carry over into the auditory and kinesthetic systems, get a sense of playing a tape or record backwards, or 'walking through' (even acting out) backwards, do aim for high speed though.

5) *'Install' the new, empowering, Biblical alternative and condition the new pattern in until it is consistent:* now we have 'taken the old CD out' we are ready to replace it with a new one. You know it's time to do this because, if you have calibrated to the 'problem' – how the person looks as they

start to access that state – you will now see that the person is not able to 'get back' the problem, or it is now a mixed state, either simultaneously, so the problem seems to have incongruity, or sequentially where the problem would trigger off the feelings of the 'interrupt' and therefore would be incomplete. There are several ways to redirect the brain and install a new 'programme' of thinking / feeling / behaving; you could use the 'strategies' approach, where, if you have taken note of how they do the problem e.g. 'see X, feel Y, say to myself Z, go do problem behaviour', now you have ruined the old sequence you can add a new piece, anytime after the stimulus (X), you can change the internal feeling (use an anchor, or mixed associations), or change the internal dialogue, and the behaviour will be entirely different. To condition it in you need two things – repetition and intensity, if you think back to how neuro-associations are formed, you remember that the more intensely emotional or pleasurable a thing was, the stronger the neural connection, we can now use this for our benefit. Speed in the repetition is important too,the rest of this chapter is adapted from a live training which I opened with:

'We are going to learn more this evening than you could hope for, and the wonderful thing is, is that you don't need to try to remember it at all.' What I mean by that is, everything that happens to you is recorded fully on the hard disk of your brain (obviously not everything that happens around you, because there are the constraints of your physical abilities, like whether you have good or poor eyesight & hearing, and also the fact that you have to ignore the majority of things going on or you would just BOOOM! Overload!) But have you ever noticed that you hear or see something and then that's it, it's lost? But maybe years later someone mentions it, and as they give a little detail it all comes rushing back? So you didn't forget it, you just hadn't recalled it, but given the time when you needed that information again you were able to get it back again.

I would suggest a parallel with what Jesus said when he promised the disciples that the Holy Spirit would bring them remembrance of what he had taught them, it did not mean that they would have to keep trying to remember what he had said, feeling anxious that they would forget, but that the Holy Spirit would supernaturally bring that accurate and undistorted recall to them so that the gospels we have are true and reliable. In a much less significant way, we are going to learn and experience some new things that you don't need to try and remember because you will find that they become available as and when you need them.

'Right, how many of you have had your telephone number changed? Can you remember it? Can you remember your old one? It's a little harder but you can can't you, so how do you do that? Its amazing to think that when you ask your brain for your phone number it gives you the right one, that's because your brain usually codes more recent learning with a higher coding than old information. I say usually, because exceptions are along the lines of when we learn something in an intensely emotional state, say something irrational, it is quite hard to just "talk someone out of it" with new accurate information because that state interferes, so we have another way of doing that.'

But just think if your brain didn't keep updating what you have learned in this way, you wouldn't believe you could jump a 3 foot puddle, because there was a time when you were 18 months old when you couldn't! OK, so new learning is a sign of growth, of being alive, and so in one sense we can see all change as new learning, we used to respond in one way, then we learned a new phone number and now we respond another way: the 'old number' is not erased, because when you try you can recall it, so you have the choice of dialling it if you want, but your brain says 'why bother, I don't live there anymore' so your brain has found a new route to 'phone home'

All change is learning and we learn quick and easy, how about if we had a conversation one word a day, or we saw a movie one frame a week, it wouldn't make sense, our brains process information very fast, and that is how we learn and therefore change. There are two basic kinds of change, there is 'remedial' i.e. applying a remedy, so you're 'broken', you come to me and I fix you, now if that was a physical thing like a broken bone then you could go and break it again and so we could have a long and unproductive relationship. The second kind is called 'generative' because it is something that sets you up for the future in a new way, and is more like flicking over the first domino and then all the others go over, or the ripples on a pond after you have dropped just one pebble in it. So if I could teach you to have strong leg muscles, to be careful with yourself, to avoid environments where legs get broken, etc., where even if you encountered the situation you would be greater than the leg breaking force and would overcome it and not need fixing, generative is more a direction than a cure, instead of asking 'what's wrong, how can I fix it?', generative change asks, 'what's great, how can I make it better still?' When we are considering our own personal growth and development or helping to counsel or disciple someone else, Christlikeness offers us the most generative direction of all.

Interestingly, in the process of remedial change we often learn things that are useful for the future and we use them generatively, i.e. when we did the backward movie and association / dissociation they were primarily remedial, dealing with your past, but you learnt that you could take control of what you do inside your head and that learning sets you in a new direction. This all sounds very highbrow stuff, but we can look at scripture and see that God does both kinds of change: in salvation, we are broken, sinful, hellbound and separated from him, and through Jesus he rescues us, forgives us, and 'fixes' us, and then in the generative sense, He makes us His children, and adopts us, and sets us the new direction of maturing in our sonship so we become more like Jesus, and at this point I hope you will see that we have gone full circle from where we started from, we are truly children of God, and all change is to be in the direction of Christlikeness, whether that is in being saved, or in developing in the fruit of the Spirit in Galatians 5.22-23.

Now let's consider how we can use what we have learnt about learning in the light of growing as Christians: one way to tackle the future is to take a 'resource' and 'future pace' it, i.e. know what's coming up, know what you have had as a resource in the past and link them up in advance, for example, if you created an anchor of: knowing God's presence and faithfulness, confidence, joy, gratitude and energy and vitality, and thought ahead of a panel coming up, or something else that caused anxiety will triggering that feeling, then you have linked the two in advance. Paul actually demonstrates how he has hope for the future, even in coming troubles, because his hope is built on past experiences of God's faithfulness and power, you can read this in Rom 5.1-5.

The first way to 'install' is the *'swish pattern'* which consists of finding a cue image or situation that would lead you off into thinking or behaviour that you don't want, and changing the association so it takes you in a direction you do want.

'So first of all think of a situation that fits this description........ get a cue image, bring it up big and bright, now put that to one side for a moment and make a big bright image of the kind of person you want to be: now let's digress a little, I would like you to make a composite image, and let's work on it together for a while, of what you think a child of God looks like, not outwardly, but in terms of character, speech, reactions, the way you would walk, the way that you resemble Jesus in your manner with others (a brainstorming session describing an attractive Christian life), now I would like you to find a way of representing that in your image of yourself, maybe the way you are standing, or a sparkle in your eyes, a calmness and trust in your bearing as you look at this image of what you want to become as you grow and change as a Christian, remember you will be able to update this as you learn more about being like Jesus, notice how this makes you feel, it is compelling, it draws you to it, it pulls you in a new direction.

Ok, so do you think it would be useful to be able to link the cue image that used to take you off into sinful, or unhelpful behaviour and thinking, to link this image with a new one that pulled you towards a happy holiness and a calm trust in God? that every time you encountered this problem it would remind you that you are a new creation and the old things have passed away? and even your problems would become a stimulus to propel you in the right direction rather than causing you to stumble?'

Steps in the swish pattern:

a) Bring up the cue image
b) Place the desired image in the corner, small and dark, and then make the desired image grow in size and brightness, coming closer and breakthrough the first picture,

c) As it grows make the sound 'whoooosh!', when it breaks through feel the feelings associated with looking at that compelling image of how you want to be and respond. Essentially what you are doing is through repetition and emotional intensity you are telling your brain 'see this (image 1) – do this (image 2)'

Ok, now do this fast 10 times ...

now think of the cue image, what happens? Aha! a new learning!

The second method of 'installation' is by *anchoring:* 'If we elicit a strong resource state and anchor it, we can turbocharge our installation, as the person thinks of how they will now respond in the situation that would have caused them a problem in the past, we can fire off the anchor and say 'Now, as you feel these feelings, notice how you respond differently, what choices you now have available to you as you take this resource with you.' What we are doing here is replacing or changing the see / feel component of a strategy because with the resource anchor we can go "see the old trigger; feel these new empowering feelings ... how do you choose to respond now?"'

A third way of installation is by storytelling and 'stacking' metaphors (like stacking pancakes, layer upon layer). This section has been an example of stacking, with multiple illustrations and allusions, which repeat and rehearse the pattern, go back over this section again and notice how many there are.

Because we are motivated away from pain and towards pleasure, in the leverage we have activated this system, let's enhance it by giving *rewards*; chunk down to small, achievable (believable) successes and reinforce yourself for them, give yourself credit, treat yourself in appropriate ways – think now of a list of 10 things you can do that make you feel good, and are good for you, and reward yourself for your successes, don't put it all off into the future, or you will 'stir up the wrath of your secondary gain!'

Another way to reinforce and condition the changes is to chunk up the *meanings and values* of the changes you have made, move up the logical levels to make it fit identity, you have given up smoking (level of behaviour) but as a behaviour you could start again, if however you chunk up to identity as a non-smoker, it is incompatible with who you are to take on that behaviour again – up the stakes, it really will work for you. We have the strongest card here because we are children of the Living God, and temples of the Holy Spirit.

6) **Future pace:** the last thing we do, although we will have been doing it to an extent in an ongoing way is to check out what we have done. Firstly, test ecology although we have used the well-formed outcome questions, make sure that the changes are fully appropriate across all the contexts of the persons life, check for the sense of peace which functions as an umpire over our lives (Col 3.15). The test in the future, make sure that what you think you have done works! don't be shy of trying it out, I would rather find out that we weren't quite finished *before* the person goes and falls on their face! Test your work thoroughly, you owe it to the people you help. Finally, to have them transformed in your office, but still struggling outside would be worse than useless so bridge the changes over to the 'real world', here are some future paces that will help you do these three things:

- 'As you imagine yourself in the future in a situation that might have caused you to "X" in the past, step into a movie of that and see how differently you are now behaving and feeling, hear what you are now saying to yourself (and notice how well you are handling this now).'

- A lovely one from Richard Bandler: 'What will it be like, having made those changes now …, in the future …, as you look back and see what it was like to have had those problems…, as you think about that now?' Sounds weird, but it gives the person the chance to step into the future and gain hindsight wisdom on the changes already made – very powerful indeed.

We can also use *timelines,* get the person to make a rich and compelling, *associated* picture of themselves having dealt with the problem and it being 'no big deal', have them float up out of their timeline taking the picture with them, and ask them to insert it where it is most appropriate in their future, but as they let it drop down into their timeline they step out from it, and dis-associate, so in one sense it become a 'future memory', interest-ingly if you ask them what happens as they do this, the events leading up to and subsequent from that new memory on the timeline adjust themselves to allow it to happen, and many times the real event takes place almost identically to the imagined memory.

Hands on

- If you haven't already, go back and do a 'swish' pattern, and see how effective it is.

- Familiarise yourself with the pain and pleasure inducing questions, and the structure of the 'Dickens' pattern, notice how these can be used conversationally.

- Think back to any times you have tried to help someone make changes, whether successfully or not, and go through this checklist and notice which elements you had, and didn't have .... what useful things do you learn from this?

Checklist: Rapport

Present state / desired state / well-formed outcome	
Leverage	
Interrupted limiting pattern	
Replace with Biblical alternative & condition	
Test & Future pace	

Chapter 12

Conclusion: A challenge to excellence

If you had visited planet earth 200 years ago and then returned at the present time, you would see the improved standards of living and anticipate that everyone would be happy and content, yet the Western world especially is mired in vain busy-ness and narcissism. Technology and communications have changed the world in so many ways people are anxious and uncertain, but the Church has the answer, some things have changed, God has not! We have the tools to enable us to confidently apply God's truth to the needs of our society, to bring more of his kingdom power to bear on this world, and also to have the strategies we need for 'guarding our hearts with all diligence' so we are not caught out and made ineffective by taking on the wrong thinking of the world.

With what we know about modelling, about how to really 'get inside' another person's experience, especially Jesus', our lives can show how good it is to know God. We have the wisdom now that comes from understanding the logical levels, the different perceptual positions, and the power of our own emotional state. In the meta-model we have a new tool to help us understand and apply the Bible. We also have a map to help us help others to make the best kind of changes in their lives.

In short, we are faced with the challenge of excellence – we have the compelling vision to be like Jesus, we have the opportunity to lay aside the things that have been in the way, and get about the Father's business.

By now you will have a framework and appreciation of the tools and skills that come from neuro-linguistics, now I would like to challenge you to be and do all the Father created you for (Eph 2.10). The remainder of this book is the toolbox section, where you will be able to develop and hone your skills. When Jesus worked as a carpenter, it is fair to assume He had to train and work hard like everyone else – if you are to work with the Word of God and the souls of men, strive for excellence, study, read, get training.[10] There is an excitement and a privilege being about the Fathers business, there is also tremendous responsibility – I pray that you will rise to it. Some people express concern that these techniques can be manipulative, yes they can – all technology and knowledge can be misused, so we are all the more accountable and are to be more responsible. In the rapport skills section we learn how to 'manipulate' ourselves so we can communicate and understand most effectively – we do not manipulate a Frenchman by learning to speak French, we increase our flexibility and put the onus on us to reach out to others as Jesus did.

In my experience, neuro-linguistics can be applied in just about every area where there is communication and subjective experience. I encourage you to work through the exercises with use and application in mind, I have used these models in at least the following areas:

1) *parenting*, (and teaching a 'Positive Parenting' course over the last few years), particularly the skills of pattern interrupt's, storytelling, pleasure and pain reinforcements, perceptual positions, and some anchoring.

2) *preaching*, although NLP will never replace prayerful dependence on God, it can aid delivery of God's message in terms of multi-sensory language, use of metaprogrammes (especially towards and away from), spatial and tonal anchoring, chunking skills – both up and down, and overcoming 'stagefright' using the phobia cure, circle of excellence and future pacing.

3) *evangelism*, the Church Growth Movement is all in favour of removing unnecessary barriers to a person receiving the gospel – we can use not only the tools under 'preaching' but also rapport, matching, mirroring, but also reframing objections and precision to help collapse unreal objections to the claims of Christ.

4) *changework*, the main thrust of this book has been changework – Western culture is increasingly stressed, anxious, dissatisfied and wanting change, there are many opportunities to get involved and represent the Kingdom of our loving God.

5) *relationships*, we can improve our own and others relationships by using the precision model to reduce mindreading and misunderstandings, also to have the flexibility to assume positive intentions. Use the beliefs, values and rules skills to further reduce conflict, and there are a host of tools here to use for changing peoples associations about each other.

6) *stress management* and enhancing the quality of life, I have done no end of stress counselling and have found using the diagnostic skills a good place to start, then scrambling the internal representations, and replacing the old state with a more empowering one by use of the 'morning questions' – teach this to the person and you will improve their life, there is a saying that goes, *'Give a man a fish and you have fed him for a day, teach a man to fish and you have fed him for a lifetime.'* If we take the time to explain a little of what we are doing, we equip people to move on from remedial change and become whole and healthy individuals..

Respond to the Call: Most of the disciples were 'stuck' in one way or another when Jesus called them, the challenge you face is to wholeheartedly follow Jesus, to embark on the adventure of discipleship, and to be transformed into his likeness. I urge you to make that decision now if you have not made it yet, follow him and master the art of loving. With all that we know, we have a responsibility to live in the good of it. Our world is desperate and the time is right for us as God's people to rise up and take our place, to shine as stars in this dark and confused time. Let Jesus become your obsession, and Christlikeness your goal, as you look back in the future on the decisions and changes you are making now, you will be glad you followed Jesus. We should never be discouraged when we discover how far short we are from being like Jesus, don't lose heart and throw in the towel. Our very lack of progress can build a stronger sense of longing in us for Gods power, and frustration with the old ways of living.

Not only that, when we fail it can prevent us from drifting away into the self-sufficiency which alienated the Pharisees from the power and life they needed. A holy life isn't our being polite with God, but is when we enter into His work of shaping and sculpting salvation out of the unlikely materials of our experience. Fr L. Gonsales says 'Because of his unlimited love, God gives us Jesus not only as a model but as a brother and a friend. The "Way" to our constant and never ending inprovement is not a religious cult, or a new ethic, or a psychotherapeutic programme – the "Way" is a person. Our "Way" to personal excellence is a brother to us, a brother who loves each of us, and wants to be our friend.'

Amen – let that be your experience.

Appendices

The Toolbox section

Three weeks of fun!

NLP has been called an attitude and methodology that leaves behind it a trail of techniques. The people who really master using the techniques will have a flexibility and tenacity, a sense of playful curiosity and respect for the person they are seeing. Some of these techniques will appear to work like 'magic', practise them thoroughly and use them to serve God. To help you 'chunk down' and begin to enjoy mastering each skill-set, I have grouped them into twenty-one days' worth of practice. Some of the techniques are presented first as a transcript of a real encounter, this is so you can notice what I do, then imagine hearing yourself saying it – 'try it on', then study it and notice the structure and flow of the intervention. Ready for some fun? Read on ....

Day 1

Goal setting

Precision is a major key in goal setting.

    1) think of something you want

    2) imagine what it would be like to have it

    3) check that it's ok for you to have it

    4) think about how it will come about

    5) focus your mind upon your goal regularly

10 steps of successful goalsetting:

1)   Ask yourself 'what do I really want' brainstorm, be free of restraint, what would I do if I knew I couldn't fail? Family, relationships, career, spirituality, skills, money, character, contribution, health, education: what would you do if the world was going to end in a week? Really vividly imagine what it would be like VAK. Einstein said, 'Imagination is more important than knowledge.'

2) Prioritise, find your top 3

3) Imagine having achieved one of these goals, and ask yourself, 'What will having this goal give me?' Discover your values, what's important to you? e.g. security / respect, not money (value elicitation) *any goal you have is just a way of fulfilling your values*
What's important to me about all these values: A CORE VALUE

4) Your life's purpose: all great achievers have a definite purpose, how things really fit together, money is not an end in itself, at the end of your life, what do you wish you have done more of 'the best things in life are not things.'
Ask yourself, what do you love to do so much that you would pay to do it, what do you feel passionate about, what would you choose to do if you have unlimited financial wealth, who are the people who are your heroes or role models now or from history, if you could achieve anything what would it be? Your life's purpose needn't be to change the world, but to be a good citizen & parent, etc.

5) How will you know when you've achieved your goal? Be specific and have a sensory based validation procedure. this will help you know whether you are getting nearer or further away. Don't just put it all off into the future, you need to have signposts along the way, not just so you know your on track but also because you don't want to put happiness off too far into the future! What are some of the smaller steps?

6) An appropriateness check (ecology) is it for your good and beneficial to others, what good is business success if it's at the expense of your health, also check that the goals are under your control and don't all depend on other people changing or doing things to make you happy. Something that you directly make happen. check out any secondary gain, and also make sure they are your goals, not your parents!

7) Timeline of events, sequence. put a time label on the top 3, then working back from your outcome, work out the major events on the way as you work backwards (use submodalities). Install the major events in appropriate places on your timeline as you daydream it.

8) Stop and ask yourself, 'What's likely to get in the way of me achieving my goal?' anticipate and pre-empt problems: lack

of specialised knowledge, space, time, confidence? Reputation? Get the benefit of hindsight in advance. Ask yourself, 'What am I going to need to do in order to overcome these obstacles, who will I need to become? Character traits? Handle these problems now. Think of times in the past when you have exhibited those traits or imagine what it would be like if you had it all now, and see how you would approach the problems with those resources

9) Make a list of all the resources, like packing for a holiday, enjoy it all: like friends, skills, education, finances, health, time, character traits, where you live, telephone (world communication), transport.

10) Take those different goals and design them into your ideal day: how does it start, people around you where you go, things you have, how you feel, design it perfectly, so it feels really good, what are some of the things that let you know how successful you are?

Day 2

Defining your Mission statement:

Take the time to look over your roles (e.g. Father, husband, child of God, church worker, British citizen, etc.), responsibilities (at home, work, church, community) and then your core values and take time to formulate a 'mission statement.' Take up to 100 words to describe what you stand for, what is essential to you and what you are committed to being and achieving in your life.

Day 3

Submodality exercises:

Problem solving technique: a good one to hard wire in! When you feel bad or find yourself focusing on something unresourceful ...

1) Stop, and allow an image to come to mind

2) What's the intention of the image? it is an action signal, what does it want me to know?

3) Think of all the things you can do to respond intelligently to the action signal

4) Drain all the colour out of the picture, shrink it at move it off into the distance.

[For these exercises find a quiet place where you can fully participate and gain the full benefit of the time you spend. The later techniques build on the principles of the earlier exercises: make a point of looking 'through' the content of the words and finding the structure and process of each intervention, for some I give you a brief summary. Notice how transferable and teachable they are, use them first on yourself and then on those who will be helped most by them. I use excerpts of client interviews so they have a 'live' feel. when there is a series of dots in the text (......) it indicates a pause. Remember – look for the process and the structure, and enjoy!]

Day 4

Movie music: find a mildly unpleasant memory, one that can still give you a slight kinaesthetic response. Now run it through with some 'sound track' I like to use the theme music from *Indiana Jones*, you may want *Star Wars*, William Tell Overture, circus music or the 'Birdie Song'. Notice how this changes your state as you review your memory – this is a useful auditory component you can use to either diminish unpleasant feelings, or try this. Think of a 'successful' memory, and gain a little of the feeling, now add some strong 'hero' sound track, something that you really like and that adds to the good feelings, notice the changes it makes – now think of something you would like to go well in the future, maybe something you feel a little nervous about – run through the movie of how you would like it to go, and add the 'movie music' of success, notice again how it helps associate the right kinds of feelings to that future event.

Picture framing: this is the visual equivalent of movie music, find a mildly unpleasant memory as before, this time freeze frame it at a point that represents the whole memory to you. Put the picture in a frame, would you like one with gold leaves swirling around it? A modern chrome one? How about a pink fluffy one with Dalmatian spots? Also would you like the picture in colour or black and white? How would it look if it was painted in oils? As a Renoir? Picasso?! Or done in pastels? Experiment with favourite artists styles (I like water colours or Van Gogh's Sunflowers style). Of course it is perfectly OK to combine movie music and picture framing. I often like to add that there can be a small brass plate screwed onto the picture frame which has the learning they can make or have made from the experience, they may not quite be able to read it, but there is something there to be learned so history does not repeat itself.

Day 5

Association / disassociation patterns: The more you experiment with these the more powerful you will realise they are, and the way to use them is simple: pull up a pleasant memory, look at it, get a sense of it and then 'step into it' see what you saw at the time, hear what you heard, breath the way you were breathing at the time, notice how that feels. Now pull up an unpleasant memory, have a look at it and get a sense of it, and now 'step out of it' make sure you see yourself in the picture over there, hear any sounds as they come from over there, back then, feel the distance between you and that event, even push it away so it is smaller and more distant. With practice we can do this easily, if a person has difficulty disassociating from a memory, get them to practise (it is a skill) by imagining looking into a mirror and seeing themselves in the mirror, this overcomes the oddness of seeing themselves in a memory.

Falling in and out of love: when we fall in love we do not write a pros and cons list of the attributes of the person we love, rather, we notice and associate into all the things we love about the person, and disassociate from any things which we wouldn't like about them (love is not blind, it is just very selective). Over time, however, the intensity of pleasure may diminish from the things we have associated into, and also we have started noticing the things we had previously deleted. Real trouble starts when we associate into the things we don't like, no matter how trivial (toothpaste tube caps and toilet seats!) and are now disassociated from the things we love about the person. This doesn't mean we don't love the person, we just are not focusing on things that make us act loving, love has got buried.

To sort this out we have to ask, 'What was it that I really loved about this person when we first met? what was it all about? how did I feel about them then? (feel it) pull up a set of five or six representations of the things you love about them, run them past fast, bring them closer and then step into them, reassociate into them, do this three or four times (once you have stepped into them, do not step out again, or you are doing a backwards swish on them!) draw the closer and closer (usually our brains code closeness in proximity with recency in time). Now for the other part, pull up a set of the representations of the things that bug you, run then past in front of you, step out of each of them and push them further and further away, do this until they are distant and feel unconvincing. If we will deliberately associate into the things we love and disassociate from anything negative, we will stay in loving states, this will lead to loving behaviours – how can you go wrong?

The alternative to this is if for some reason you are in love with someone (or something) you shouldn't be, reverse it, disassociate from any pleasant experiences you had together and then fully associate into all the unpleasant or difficult times, run them by fast and in colour, closer and closer so you feel you have reached 'threshold' and have had enough. (Make sure you get these the right way round!) this is a general pattern that can be used for many problems, it is a powerful way of associating pain and pleasure in our nervous system. The reason fro speed is that our visual representations move faster than our kinaesthetic response, so we are able to crank it up like on a ratchet so we can push responses we don't want through threshold, then they don't work properly anymore, this is especially useful with food cravings, etc.

Steps: recall pleasant, positive memories, or the attributes you like about the person, associate into them, recall the things you don't like, dissociate from them.

Day 6

Intensifying and diminishing kinesthetics: pleasure. when building a strong resource anchor it is helpful to access some really strong states, but what if the person doesn't seem to have any? Do this, bring up a pleasant memory and disassociate from it, take some time to enhance the sbmd's to intensify it – bring it closer, make it clearer, in colour, 3D, unframed, as a movie, enhance the sound – make it louder, closer, stereophonic, rhythmic and resonant, when it looks and sounds compelling to the person, have them step into it. 'See what you saw at the time, hear what you heard, breath and stand as you did / would, etc.'

Now for the fun bit, to really crank it up, once they are experiencing the first level kinesthetics say, 'Now, in a moment I am going to ask you to notice a small sparkling dot slightly to one side or the other of what you can see, can you see it yet? In just a moment that sparkling dot is going to expand and open up like the iris in your eye, and as it does it will enhance all of the *sbmds*, and I want you to step through the iris into the picture again and double those feelings .... see the iris open up, that's right, step through and feel those feelings double, now' repeat this a couple of times and anchor it. You will notice breathing and skin colour, etc., change dramatically as the kinesthetics 'catch up' with the internal representations. This can be used with any state you want to anchor, confidence, 'sizzle', determination, decisiveness, joy, peaceful trust, etc. I have found this useful in sexual counselling to help those whose nervousness interferes with lovemaking to reassociate into 'being there' (instead of talking to themselves about how uptight they are!)

> [N.B. this is a good one for you to practise your calibration skills on – watch their breathing, skin tone, lower lip size and muscle tension.]

Pain: as I've said before, pain often is a message which we ignore at our peril, but there is a category of pain which can ecologically be removed or diminished, of course we need to deal sensibly with the message and any secondary gain issues, also to make sure that we refer people to a medical doctor. Sometimes by simply translating pain into a different sensory system we can manipulate it so it becomes manageable. Couple this with the knowledge that we get more of what we focus on and also we are able to be 'interrupted' out of some pain, especially 'hysterical' pain.

An example: a man came to me with pain in his shoulder, where a crate had fallen on him, the doctor had treated it, but the pain seemed to be disproportionate to the injury .... 'OK, what I'd like you to do is to close your eyes for a moment and really concentrate on that pain, can you do that? Tell me, if the pain was a colour, what colour would it be? (black) excellent, and what kind of shape would it be if you could see it? (Spider shaped with sharp hooks on the end of each leg), now is there anything else, now you look at it, is it uniform in its colour (the centre was a very dark red). Now if those colours and shapes were a sound, what would they be? (A rat or bird of prey screeching – the pain was steady but with intermittent sharp stabs), ok now I would like you to imagine being in your kitchen, can you do that? good, now in your minds eye, walk over and turn in the cold water tap – not so fast you nearly splashed me! (laughter), that's it, so it's just running steadily down the sink, now go to the drawer where you keep the scissors and go back to the sink, with the scissors in your other hand I want you to lean right over the sink and snip off the end of one of those spider legs, good, now lean right over the sink so as that blacky red liquid starts to empty out, it gets washed away, don't spill any because it might stain, now, imagine that each of those strands were toothpaste tubes, just roll them out and squeeze out any residue pain, take all the time you want ..... ok, all out? You sure? Where's the pain? (surprised laughter "Its gone!").

What I did here is make a visual representation and then change that representation, the unconscious mind understood what to do to equate that with pain reduction. An important thing is to use whatever metaphors or descriptions the person offers you, and experiment, see if you can increase and decrease sensations. Milton Erickson was once asked to work with a man who had phantom limb pain, in his own peculiar way he saw limb pain as a skill, so he asked how much phantom limb pleasure the man would rather feel!

Steps: the secret is to move the person out of the kinesthetic system (where the pain is) using overlap, visual is best because it seems 'furthest away'. Use the client's own description and metaphor to diminish the sensations – remember pain has a purpose, a message which must be dealt with.

Day 7

Memory management: if we now put some of these things together we can have an effective way of sorting our memories. I have done the following with many people, but particularly those who suffer from mild depression or have a glum and pessimistic bias. To be able to maintain that perspective (which is not accurate) they must disassociate from pleasant experiences, and associate into painful ones -these are the people who, even if you see them laughing and having a good time will tell you 'but on the inside I was crying!' I like to use the metaphor of tidying bookshelves, when we are sorting them out we don't have to open and read every book before we can move it, similarly when we are rearranging our memory files, we don't have to re-experience them – especially the negative ones.

First we get up a pleasant memory and enhance it using submodalities, and then step into it, so that it is fully associated. Next, pull up an unpleasant memory, and using submodalities, decrease its intensity, then 'picture frame' it and disassociate from it, so there is no emotion left attached at all, an important thing to do is to make sure that you do the piece about the nameplate where the learning and wisdom that can be gained from the experience is available to us, without the pain. Now using either timelines or just a simple request, have the person float back to a very early time in their life, and to drop down into their timeline and reformat every negative and painful experience disassociated, framed and with the learning available moving forward in time through early childhood, school years, etc., and that the unconscious mind is able to understand what it is to do, even though the conscious mind is not able to fully keep up, ask them to take a deep breath and open their eyes when they have got to the present. Now have them again go back and starting from the same point in their personal history, to reformat every pleasant and positive memory as enhanced and fully associated and again to move forward through time up until the present and open their eyes. This gives people a chance to have all their unpleasant past as the basis for wisdom and learning and not as a source of pain or discomfort, and all the positive past as a treasure house of good feelings and optimism. This does not in any way change the content of the memories, what has happened has really happened, but that's the point – only in our minds can we feel as if it is still happening, this is where we can effect powerful change that releases a lot of energy that was being squandered on the past.

Having explained this to the people who have been through this process I often future pace them to see if they like the impact of organising their memories this way – I have never yet had anyone want to change it back! My experience has been that people sleep very soundly when they go to bed on the night of this procedure, also that 'forgotten' memories bubble up over subsequent weeks, as painful memories can now be integrated and faced without trauma. Occasionally people will choose a strongly negative memory to use as the format pattern, if this happens you will want to use the phobia cure and ask them to choose a different mildly unpleasant memory for the formatting example.

Steps: create an associated, compelling and rich format/pattern of submodalities, ask the unconscious mind to float back to the beginning of the persons timeline, and reformat every positive and enjoyable memory in this way, moving towards the present time.

Next create a dim, distant, silent and dissociated format, ask the unconscious mind to do the same for all negative, traumatic and painful memories, making sure to preserve all learnings that will serve you in the future.

Day 8

Timelining negative emotions: timeline therapy is a whole area in its own right, and I recommend you read the books in the bibliography, but just so you can get a taste of how powerful this technology is, do this exercise. First identify a negative emotion that limits your present behaviour or just stops you being the person you believe God wants you to be. Give that feeling a name, maybe fear, anger, sadness, guilt etc., and realise that there was a time in your life when you had not ever felt that feeling. 'Now, what I'd like you to realise is that the feelings of (anger) that you have been feeling have been connected to other significant and intense experiences of anger too, see through your life you have learned anger, and how to feel like that and when you feel anger at something happening in the present, you access all those other times too – have you noticed that sometimes you overreact to what is happening in the now because of unsorted anger in the past? (yes) OK, good … now I'd like you to close your eyes and just get in touch with your timeline, kind of where it is … and now just float up or away from it so you can just see it right down there … and I'd like to ask that part of you that knows ... if you knew the root cause of that negative emotion, which when you disconnect from it, will cause the negative emotion to disappear when would that be? (I was about four years old) ... now, I'd like to ask you to float back to just after that time, keeping your distance from it, and now with your back to the present I want you to look down and back at that event about fifteen minutes after it happened ... and with the benefit of that hindsight, but not feeling bad, I'd like your unconscious mind to take all the things that could and should be learned from this event and store them securely in the place where those learnings are best kept, to increase your wisdom and help you in your daily life, and which will allow you, now, to fully let go of all those negative feelings ... now I would like you to float directly above the event and look down at it, and again to preserve the learnings you get from this perspective ... and now, I would like you to move to a position at least fifteen to thirty minutes before this first event and turn around so you are looking down at it, but also to look forward across it towards the present and the future ... and now, before that event had ever happened, I'd like you to ask yourself the question 'where are those negative feelings now?' (laughter, 'they haven't happened yet, they're not there!') ... OK, from this position I'd like to ask that part of you which knows there were things to be learned so history is not repeated, are there any other learnings to be made? ('no', if there had been ask that part to make all other learnings that will enable the person to fully let those feelings go, etc.), now from that position, just release all those negative feelings, just let them go ... (long pause) ... do you believe that even back then God knew about you and loved you and wanted the best for you? (yes), in that case I'd like you to become aware of God's love and wholeness surrounding and touching and healing you now and back then, notice how different it would have been if you had known then what you know now ... and now I would like you to move forward in time towards the present only as fast as you can allow all other events with similar emotions to release them fully so you can find them gone completely, and take all the time you want because at this level of experience there is no time ... now I'd like you just to go back and drop down into any of those events, maybe especially the first one ... how does that feel? (It doesn't..it's ok). I then future paced what formerly had triggered the feelings of rage and anger, and the person found completely different responses available.

A similar thing can be done with limiting decisions which can be re-evaluated in the light of scripture and Gods love and acceptance of them, obviously where wrong has been done it needs to be confessed to God, and sometimes restitution made. There are many applications of timeline therapy (as many as there are instances of our past getting in the way!), I have also used it with people with addictions, where we have been able to disconnect them emotional component of the habit, and then go back and re-evaluate the decisions which were made at the root cause. We are careful not to 'change history' only to learn from it, and make sure we don't repeat it.

Day 9

Phobia cure: if a person has severe trauma or a phobic response (an intense physical reaction) then we are not able to just alter submodalities because the person will 'step into' the horrid memory and freak out! to get round this we use 'double disassociation'. This is one of the things that made neuro-linguistics famous, the 'six minute phobia cure', to be honest if there are no issues of secondary gain I have to ask 'why take so long?' This can be done using timelines, above the timeline pulling up a traumatic memory, but unless I have already done timeline elicitation with a person I will do it like this. Before I do this I always set a strong, positive 'bail out' anchor in case they start to associate in to the trauma, if you ever forget and it happens, just use a pattern interrupt, get them to stand up, open eyes, walk around your office, read the book titles on the top shelf of my book cases, etc. 'Ok I'd like you to close your eyes, take a nice deep breath in and become aware of how the chair is supporting you .... you are allowed to breath out (laughter) .... oxygen is a crucial component to all successful change! (the person then adjusts position and looks less tense) now, have you ever been in one of those new long duration cinemas? You remember what colour the seats were? (I tested just to make sure it was a positive experience) just imagine that you are back there in the most comfortable seat ... that's right, now, in a moment, but not yet, the curtains are going to draw back and there will be a black and white movie of that experience, but going from a time of safety and comfort before the event, and finishing at a point of safety and comfort afterwards, do you understand? (nods) good, but before that happens I would like you to gently float up out of that you sitting comfortably in that seat and float up and back into the projectionist's booth, is that OK? Now I want you to watch that you sitting comfortably down there as she watches that movie of that other you back then, over there, do you understand? Good so press play and give me a nod when it's finished, but only watch that you down there as she watches that younger you, back then over there on the screen ... (nods) now freeze frame it at the end, and just float down to the floor and look at that you who just watched that, and notice that she has learned something of value for you, and now I want you to go up to that younger you on the screen and step into her body, see through her eyes, hear through her ears – I know nothing is happening yet because we paused it, but in just a moment we will run the whole thing backwards in full colour, really fast with words going back into people's mouths and that kind of thing until you reach the beginning point of comfort and safety, you have to get there before I can count to seven, are you ready? (Smile and nod), on your marks, get set, go! (I hum the loony toons music and finish with 'that's all folks'), great, now step out of the screen, and move over to that you sitting comfortably and then gently step into her. Just for a moment open your eyes and tell me how you feel when you think of that event ... (weird, like it's no big deal any more).'

Obviously if you don't get the result you want first time through, use different elements to scramble it, but always use double disassociation, you may even want to fire off the anchor while they are going through the backwards movie – the important thing is to test thoroughly and use your sensory acuity.

> [N.B. now go back through it and see how many times the person is dissociated, notice the structure of this one, as the principle carries through into ...]

Day 10

Scramble: you are already familiar with the basic idea and procedure of scrambling by now, here are some additional strings to your bow ... how about running the movie forward from a disassociated view, but changing speeds of central character & surrounding, have your disassociated self moving at twice the speed of the surroundings, it means that you finish first, and all the cause / effects and action / reaction links are scrambled because responses are at different times to what caused them! Now run the movie in reverse but with the situation running at double speed and yourself moving at half speed, it means the movie finishes before you do. Other things that work well are simply putting an image on the TV and then turn it off! or putting in on reinforced glass (like a car windscreen) and bashing it with a hammer, the image then 'crazes' and falls into a thousand little pieces, if you've ever seen the 'meltdown' screensaver on a computer you can do that as long as it doesn't make the image more scary (i.e. not for use on peoples faces!) The more commonplace metaphors you use to enable a person to manipulate sbmds the better, we can do a lot with TVs and videos, also make sounds come through cheap, tinny radios or a Walkman with the batteries running down.

Day 11

Swish: use this anytime there is a stimulus – response connection, it 're-routes' the stimulus to where you want to go – this is helpful for smokers and other habits. Make sure the desired state is disassociated or they will feel they have already achieved it, and is more than just doing something else, make it a representation of 'the kind of person you would be for whom this wouldn't even have been a problem'. Experiment with finding the submodality 'drivers' for most it is closeness and brightness, or a change in location.

Day 12

Motivation / attraction: use the sbmd lists to elicit the difference between what is motivating and compelling to a person, and what is not, then have the person map over those qualities to what they know they should do but never get around to, notice the shifts in physiology, you will also see which are the 'driver' sbmds in this exercise. This can be used to change from unmotivated to motivated (or vice versa if appropriate), uncertain to certain, confused to understanding etc. Also look at the gestures and minimal cues that indicate where a person is placing their timeline and internal pictures in the 'personal space' around them, this will give the opportunity to change internal experience from the outside – Bandler jokingly says 'Keep your submodalities to yourself .... or the're mine!'

Day 13

Visual squash : this is great if you have a parts conflict, where both parts are valid, and you don't want to do a six-step reframe. Firstly clarify (using meta-model questions) the conflict and the 'parts' involved, then ask the person to make a visual representation of each part and place one part in each hand, this can be a face, activity or simply a colour, as long as it symbolises the part fully. Now 'chunk up' in your language until you have found the positive intention that both parts have, the further you chunk up, the vaguer and more abstract it will seem. What resources does each part have that would help the other part be more effective in fulfilling its positive intention? 'Now, if the part in one hand was red, and in the other hand blue, in your minds eye allow them to arc up in a rainbow to a level just below your eyeline .... and as they meet they become a perfect new colour, and notice now how the colour seeps down each side so they fully grade into and metamorphose into one another ..... as a full integration of these parts takes place now ..... I would like you to notice how this new part fulfils the positive intention of both the old conflicting parts in a most elegant way ..... and now allow that new part to integrate itself inside you and tell me how you feel about those choices you now have? .... (Great)

Day 14

Reframing a critical inner voice: if a person is 'tormented' with disempowering self-talk it is useful first of all to elicit the positive intention, the person probably feels so negative about their own internal dialogue that they have made it an enemy, but in reality it is probably just trying to help. Obviously one approach to take is to replace unhelpful and untrue content and replace it with an 'antidote', we can set up and fire off some powerful anchors while affirming biblical 'incantations' (phrases and slogans which become emotionally charged – that's why to make sure it is Biblical is important) or

alternatively we can play with the structure of the voice .....
'now, maintaining the positive intention of that critical voice,
but making it more possible to help fulfil its intention because
you were trying to ignore it before .... I wonder if you can
imagine that voice coming from your elbow? How about your
thumb? Now how about if it sounded like Kermit the frog? How
about if it talked nicely to you and said please? What would be
the best way to be able to hear the important message this part
has for you in a way that didn't make you feel bad?

Day 15

Six-step reframe: if a swish, timeline or sbmd change does not
seem to 'stick' then there is likely to be issues of secondary gain
or objecting parts, which feel that their positive intention is
being overlooked and therefore the change is not ecological, the
'proper' six step reframe goes like this: 1) access the part of the
person responsible for the behaviour to be changed, thank it for
what it has been doing and reassure it that what you are doing is
making sure it fulfils the benefits in the most appropriate way; 2)
make sure you have communication with the part, ask for a
system of signalling; 3) discover the benefits the part had been
trying to achieve through the behaviour; 4) ask the persons
creative part to generate at least three alternative behaviours
which would fulfil this benefit; 5) check that these alternatives
are acceptable to the original part and all other parts (if not, set
the creative part to work again, or ask them to make the necessary adjustments so that the alternatives would be ok); 6) once
this is done, future pace, have them step ten days into the future
and see that the new behaviours are natural and automatic and
fulfil their needs, then ask the original part if it will take responsibility to generate these new behaviours in the future, wait for a
'yes' response, and you're done!

Day 16

'Change' personal history: another way to handle problem
memories is to ask the person what resources they would have
needed to have handled the situation differently, in a way they
would be happy with, particularly with the wisdom they have
from hindsight. Get them to access memories with this resource
(if they say they never have had the resource use the 'as-if'

frame, get them to stand, breath, etc. as if they had the resource) and then anchor it, use sbmds to add sizzle, make sure you have a really strong stacked anchor. Ask them to go back in their mind to that (problem) experience, but this time to take back these feelings (fire off and hold anchor) ask them to notice how things would be different, what other choices they would have, and then to come forward through time if they had felt those feelings. Doing this provides a way for the person to have a kin-aesthetic sense of learning from the past, often we look back and say 'I should have, I wish I had' doing this actually makes those choices available to us in the future.

Day 17

Anchoring: first let's remember the four keys to successful anchoring 1) the person is fully associated (really there), full body experience, as intense as possible; 2) we set the anchor at the peak of the experience; 3) we use a unique trigger, preferably in more than one sensory system, so a voice tone and touch will be more effective than a visual one, especially if we will ask them to close their eyes later! 4) we will need to replicate the trigger precisely. Now let's use these skills.

Circle of excellence: think of a time in the future when you will need a particular emotions resource, say confidence or mental clarity. Remember a time when you had that resource (or create it using the as-if frame) and fully associate into the memory, feel the feelings, and as you do imagine a circle of colour around you on the floor, now step out of the circle and leave those feelings over there, if you like step back in and feel the feelings again, now step out again and think of a trigger for when you will need to feel those feelings. For me, hearing myself being introduced at a big speaking event (at this point I want to be focused on the Lord and what I am communicating, not on whether I feel self-conscious!). In your mind's eye or ear see or hear that trigger and as you do step into the circle and feel those feelings, open your eyes, break state and repeat. Do this a couple of times until just thinking of the trigger brings up the resourceful state.

> [N.B. this is only really using a spatial anchor and future pacing, but it is so effective it's amazing – how about teaching

this to your kids before they sit their exams? Also good for stage-fright.]

Stacking: When you want a particularly strong anchor, stack lots of them together, this means elicit several strong, fully associated states but anchor them on the same spot, I have found that some of the most versatile states to anchor are laughter, surprise, gratitude and confidence – these make a great 'cocktail'!

Day 18

Collapsing anchors: once you have learned to stack anchors so you have some powerful resource states available, you can elicit problem states too, and then fire them off simultaneously, this is a kinaesthetic equivalent of the visual squash, and is very powerful, hold the anchors for as long as a minute or two until the integration has completely finished, then test by firing off the 'problem' anchor, you will either get a mixed response or just the stacked anchor response. Always make sure that your stacked anchor is considerably more powerful than the problem or this will work the wrong way!

Chaining anchors: although it isn't done as much these days, you can 'chain' or sequence anchors so that they will lead from one state to another to another, for example you could help with a strategy installation by anchoring the states to back up the changes i.e. from frustration to curiosity to humour to action.

Future pacing: to set up resource anchors in the 'small talk' and rapport and information gathering part of a session, by talking about hobbies, passions, etc. means that we can use them later in future pacing and testing our work – always test anchors thoroughly, they should have measurable sensory effect, they do not belong in the land of make-believe.

Day 19

Perceptual positions: the 'autobiography' is a very gentle way of helping someone have an accurate self image – by letting them have an imagined experience of how others perceive them, it is told here in a story form, but you will easily recognise the switching of perceptual positions to gain and integrate new per-spective: 'OK, I'd like you to close your eyes and make yourself only as comfortable as you would like to be for these next few minutes, do you have a favourite chair in a favourite place where you like to go and reflect and gather your thoughts? (Nod) then I'd like you to imagine that you are there right now, in that comfortable and familiar place, and just imagine that you have been writing, writing about your life … and I'd like you to think of a person who has been, or maybe is in your life, who loves you … or respects you … or thinks well of you, or even just a person who you have helped in some way … can you think of someone like that? (Nod) now imagine writing something about that person, how you first met them, what you think about them … are they honest, good? Can you trust them? … now even as you pause for thought in writing this part of your life, I'd like you to ever so gently and peacefully, just float out of that you sitting comfortably and thoughtfully in that chair … and now, you won't have noticed before now, but just over to one side is a glass wall, or at least it looks like glass, but it feels warm and soft to the touch, but is very strong – in that wall is a transparent door, can you see that now? (Nod) now I want you to go through that door and close it behind you, that's right, and now look through at that you over there … and now I'd like you to become aware of the person standing next to you behind that wall—it's the person you were just writing about … look over at them, at the expression on their face as they look at that you over in the chair, see the softness around the eyes, see the warm way they look at you, hmmm? … now what I'd like you to do is to step, ever so respectfully into that person's body and look at yourself ever there through their eyes, the eyes of love, warmth, affection or gratitude, notice what they are saying to themselves about you … interesting huh? Yeah, now ever so softly, step back out of them and look at them again as they watch that you in the chair, see now how meaningful their expression is, how they love and appreciate you over there …. now with this knowledge I'd like you to go back through the door and rejoin yourself on the chair, and now write a few more things about this person who loves you, and also how they perceive you, and notice how that makes you feel ….'

I will do this a few times through until they have a favourable objective view of themselves, it also will make them more appreciative and respectful of the people they care about in their lives, and seems to gently bypass cognitive dissonance. Of course the most powerful person to do this with is Jesus, as it helps us to become more Biblical in our self image, and also helps us to see others as Jesus sees them too.

Day 20

Rapport, matching: you can do this mirroring a person on the TV but of course you don't see the responses you are eliciting, so it is best to do this in everyday life. Next time you are in a conversation with someone, notice their 'body language' i.e. position & gestures, also (more importantly) their breathing (rate & location), voice tempo and voice tone, when you have done this begin to mirror or match them and see how this affects the quality of understanding between you. Rapport is not a once-off matching, it is like a subtle and enjoyable dance between two people.

Day 21

Mental mapping: when you are talking to someone, imagine a bubble around them, and that the various things they talk about are 'post-it' notes, watch to see where they stick them. If you are after any particular states or values information pay particular attention to where they are placed. One of the easiest things you can do is locating another persons timeline by use of language and gestures. With all these things, feedback a sentence or two and put things in the same places and see how much it increases rapport – for those times when you want to break rapport, do the opposite!

Congratulations! now please, keep learning and growing, keep serving and helping others, and don't stop until you are just like Jesus!

Heb13.20-21 'May the God of peace, who through the blood of the eternal covenant brought back from the dead our Lord Jesus, that great shepherd of the sheep, equip you with everything good for doing his will, and may he work in us what is pleasing to him, through Jesus Christ, to whom be glory forever and ever. Amen.'

Note: if you intend to use these tools with others, I recommend that you receive training or certification in NLP from a proper training institution. Please e-mail me for details on ifield4861@hotmail.com, or check out Powerchange.com, who provide high quality Life Coach training in the UK from a Christian perspective.

Appendix: 'Altered States of mind'?

Throughout this book we have seen that it is normal for a person to experience many different states of mind and body, some empowering, some not, through the course of the average day, so we are faced with the initial difficulty of defining what is a 'normal' waking state. On top of this is the fact that approximately every ninety minutes, the brain and body's natural rhythm slows and we are prone to daydream and our minds wander, so we normally enter a different state of consciousness all by ourselves (the Ultradian Rhythm).

Some people have suggested using our levels of awareness of internal and external stimuli as a means of defining an 'altered' state, but again as human beings we are too fearfully and wonderfully made for this to help, sports players have to be extremely 'outside' minded to do well in a game like tennis or squash, but the scope of their focus is very narrow indeed. Conversely, have you ever driven a car down a long stretch of motorway and after a while someone speaks and you come back to attention, but all this time you have been driving safely – on 'autopilot.' Or again when watching TV many people become so involved in the programme that they lose awareness of the room they are in, others they are with, and will even experience their heart-rate speeding up at tense or exciting moments, and jump if something surprising happens. All these are examples of normal states of awareness that are in their *appropriate setting*.

The Bible has many things to say about different states of mind and awareness, in Acts 10 we have Peter in a trance and seeing a vision, we have Isaiah in the temple and seeing the Lord, we have Isaac in the fields meditating when Rebecca comes to marry him. It is obvious that the context sets the expectation of what is normal and appropriate in terms of our states, it would not be a good idea to try to cross a busy London street in the same attitude of mind as when our focus is deeply inside remembering the feelings of a pleasant memory, also it is not helpful when starting to pray to be in the heart thumping state of stage-fright!

It is useful to have an awareness that different states will be useful for different things – what if Peter had not felt like praying? It is unlikely that in the busyness of the day he would be receptive to God giving him a vision, but it is obvious that he would have been a lousy (or at least poor) fisherman and apostle if he spent all day in a trance!

This brings me to the effects of the techniques in this book, it is apparent that as we access memories, etc. our attention goes inside, and as we do this more fully our focus actually becomes those events and they become our experience again. Once or twice I have been asked about hypnosis, which is different in a specific way:

hypnosis is a particular state of mind, traditionally induced by someone else, where the focus of attention is narrowed down and the normal critical faculties of that person are put to one side, so that whatever is suggested is accepted as true. What marks out this kind of hypnotic trance as different to any other 'downtime' is i) that a longer-term trance state is aimed for, rather than being a short-term byproduct of thinking and processing, and ii) the degree of suggestibility, to an outside (human) agent. In Peter's case the trance was initiated by God, or at least used by Him, in clinical hypnosis it is induced and used by man – this shows the primary weakness and danger of it; that a person is passive, vulnerable and suggestible (of course when a person is grieving or traumatised they are highly suggestible too, trance is not the only time). It has been shown and properly documented that hypnosis can be a powerful tool to facilitate change, and there are Christian counsellors and psychologists who use it, who would say that if preceded by prayer and used within the limits of Biblical revelation it is as safe as any other counselling technique used by imperfect people.

This being said, I personally would recommend other techniques, used by Christian or professionally trained people, with a heavy reliance on the goodness and power of God.

Resources & Bibliography

I have tried as much as possible to list sources, I have also added books and tapes that have influenced me, *I do not share the views and values found in some of these books*, so I have shortlisted some I would recommend to you for further study: (those marked with a * are useful, ** doubly so)

Recommended books:

** *Users manual for the brain:* Hall & Bodenhamer: Crown House Publishing
** *Timelining:* Hall & Bodenhamer: Anglo American Book Co
− *Heart of the mind:* Andreas: Real People Press, 1989
− *NLP the new technology of achievement:* NLP Comprehensive: Morrow & Co, 1994

NLP as it was created: Bandler & Grinder:

− *Reframing:* Real People Press, 1982
− *Structure of magic:* Science & Behaviour Books, 1975
− *Patterns of Milton Erickson vol. 1:* Meta Publications: 1975
− *Frogs into Princes:* Eden Grove, 1979
− *Using your brain for a change:* Real People, 1985
− *Change your mind (and keep the change):* Andreas: Real People: 1987
− *Persuasion Engineering:* Meta publications, 1996
− *Magic in action:* Meta Publications, 1992
− *Insider guide to submodalities:* Bandler: meta
− *Time for a change:* Meta publications, 1993
− *Trance-formations:* Real People Press

Tony Robbins:

* *Unlimited Power:* Fawcett Columbine, 1986
** *Awaken the Giant Within:* Simon & Schuster, 1992

Other reading & books cited:

* *Introduction to Psychology & Counselling 2nd ed.:* Meier & Minirth: Baker, 1991
− *Free indeed:* Tom Marshall: Sovereign World, 1983
* *Christian Counselling (rev & exp.):* G. Collins: Word, 1989
− *Effective Biblical Counselling:* L. Crabb: Marshall Pickering: 1977
− *The Truth that sets you Free:* C. Urquhart: Hodder & Stoughton: 1993

- *A Guide to Pastoral Care:* R.E.O. White: Pickering, 1976
- *NLP Home Study Course:* NLP Comprehensive:
** *Introducing NLP:* O'Connor & Seymour: Harper Collins, 1990 / rev. 1993
* *Influence – science & practice, 2nd ed.:* R. Cialdini: Harper Collins, 1988
- *Beliefs: Dilts:* Meta publications
* *Provocative Therapy:* Farrelly: Meta publications
- *Roots of NLP:* Dilts: Meta
* *Changing belief systems with NLP:* Dilts: Meta
- *NLP the new art & science of getting what you want:* Harry Alder : Piatkus , 1994
- *Core Transformation:* C & T Andreas: Real People Press, 1994
- *You are the message:* Ailes: Dow Jones
* *Meta-states:* Hall: E.T. Publications
- *Stories that change people:* Gordon: NLP comprehensive
- *Mastery University manuals:* Robbins: RRI
** *Timeline therapy & the basis of personality:* James & Woodsmall: Meta
- *Advanced Timeline therapy:* James: Advanced Neuro-Dynamics
- *Becoming a ferocious presenter:* Hall: E.T.
** *Patterns for renewing the mind:* Hall & Bodenhamer: E.T.
- *Advanced language patterns mastery:* McLaughlin: Leading Edge
- *Churches with Roots:* Lukasse: Monarch
- *Victory over the darkness:* N.T. Anderson: Monarch, 1992
- *The Bondage breaker:* N.T. Anderson: Monarch, 1993
- *Born to Win (TA & Gestalt):* James & Jongeward: Addison Wesley: 1975
- *Influencing with integrity (rev):* G. Laborde: Anglo American: 1987
- *Words that change minds:* Charvet: Kendall Hunt
- *The Way:* Jones: Hodder & Stoughton
- *The Message:* Peterson: Navpress
- *Christianity the new humanism:* Packer: Word
- *Dynamics of spiritual growth:* Wimber: Hodder & Stoughton
- *Staying Sane:* Raj Persaud: Metro
- *I'm OK, you're OK:* Harris: Pan
* *Victory in Jesus:* Price: Marshalls
- *Introduction to developmental behavioural modelling:* McWhirter: NLP Comprehensive
- *Lazy Learning:* Beaver: Element
- *In the spirit of truth:* Christian: DLT
* *Mars and Venus together forever:* Gray: Vermilion
- *How real is real:* Watslawick: Vintage
** *Uncommon Therapy:* Haley: Norton
- *Why marriages succeed or fail:* Gottman: Bloomsbury

*   *Foundations for a healing ministry:* Marshall: Sovereign world
−   *Magic of NLP demystified:* Lewis: metamorphous
**   *Language of change:* Watslawick: Norton
−   *The situation is hopeless but not serious:* Watslawick: Norton
−   *Figuring out people:* Hall: Anglo American
−   *Mindlines:* Hall: E.T.
*   *Secrets of magic:* Hall: Crown House
−   *Power Evangelism:* Wimber: Hodder & Stoughton
−   *Building with bananas:* Copley: Paternoster
−   *Personal Disciplemaking:* Adsit: Here's Life
−   *God's Words:* Packer: IVP
−   *Basic Bible Studies (cassettes):* Price: CCF Tapes

GLOSSARY

Taken from NLP Practioners Manual, ©1998 - 1999 *Institute of Neuro-Semantics, and used by kind permission.* (**www.neurosemantics.com**)

Accessing Cues: How we use our physiology and neurology by breathing, posture, gesture, and eye movements to access certain states and ways of thinking. These are observable by others.

As-If Frame: To "pretend." To presuppose some situation is the case and then act upon it as if it is true. This encourages creative problem-solving by mentally going beyond apparent obstacles to desired solutions.

Analogue: An analogue submodality varies continuously from light to dark; while a digital submodality operates as either off or on, i.e. we see a picture in either an associated or dissociated way.

Anchoring: The process by which any stimulus or representation (external or internal) gets connected to and so triggers a response. Anchors occur naturally and in all representational systems. They can be used intentionally, as in analogue marking or with numerous change techniques, such as Collapse Anchors. The NLP concept of anchoring derives from the Pavlovian stimulus-response reaction, classical conditioning. In Pavlov's study the tuning fork became the stimulus (anchor) that cued the dog to salivate.

Association: Association contrasts with dissociation. In dissociation, you see yourself "over there." Generally, dissociation removes emotion from the experience. When we are associated we experience all the information directly and therefore emotionally.

Auditory: The sense of hearing, one of the basic representational systems.

Behavior: Any activity that we engage in, from gross motor activity to thinking.

Beliefs: The generalizations we have made about causality, meaning, self, others, behaviors, identity, etc. Our beliefs are what we take as being "true" at any moment. Beliefs guide us guide us in perceiving and interpreting reality. Beliefs relate closely to values. NLP has several belief change patterns.

Calibration:
Becoming tuned-in to another's state and internal sensory processing operations by reading previously observed noticed nonverbal signals.

Chunking:
Changing perception by going up or down levels and/or logical levels. Chunking up refers to going up a level (inducing up, induction). It leads to higher abstractions. Chunking down refers to going a level (deducing, deduction). It leads to more specific examples or cases.

Complex Equivalence:
A linguistic distortion pattern where you make meaning of someone else's behavior from the observable clues, without having direct corroborating evidence from the other person.

Congruence:
A state wherein one's internal representation works in an aligned way. What a person says corresponds with what they do. Both their non-verbal signals and their verbal statements match. A state of unity, fitness, internal harmony, not conflict.

Conscious:
Present moment awareness. Awareness of seven ± two chunks of information.

Content:
The specifics and details of an event, answers *what?* And *why?*

Contrasts with process or structure.

Context:
The setting, frame or process in which events occur and provide meaning for content.

Cues:
Information that provides clues to another's subjective structures, i.e. eye accessing cues, predicates, breathing, body posture, gestures, voice tone and tonality, etc.

Deletion:
The missing portion of an experience either linguistically or representationally.

Digital:
Varying between two states, a polarity. For example, a light switch is either on or off. Auditory digital refers to thinking, processing, and communicating using words, rather than in the five senses.

Dissociation:
Not "in" an experience, but seeing or hearing it from outside as from a spectator's point of view, in contrast to association.

Distortion:
The modeling process by which we inaccurately represent something in our neurology or linguistics, can occur to create limitations or resources. The process by which we represent the external reality in terms of our neurology. Distortion occurs when we use language to describe, generalize, and theorize about our experience.

Downtime:	Not in sensory awareness, but "down" inside one's own mind seeing, hearing, and feeling thoughts, memories, awarenesses, a light trance state with attention focused inward.
Ecology:	Concern for the overall relationships within the self, and between the self and the larger environment or system. Internal ecology: the overall relationship between a person and their thoughts, strategies, behaviors, capabilities, values and beliefs. The dynamic balance of elements in a system.
Elicitation:	Evoking a state by word, behavior, gesture or any stimuli. Gathering information by direct observation of non-verbal signals or by asking meta-model questions.
Empowerment:	Process of adding vitality, energy, and new powerful resources to a person; vitality at the neurological level, change of habits.
Eye Accessing Cues:	Movements of the eyes in certain directions indicating visual, auditory or kinesthetic thinking (processing).
Epistemology:	The theory of knowledge, how we know what we know.
First Position:	Perceiving the world from your own point of view, associated, one of the three perceptual positions.
Frame:	Context, environment, meta-level, a way of perceiving something (as in Outcome Frame, "As If" Frame, Backtrack Frame, etc).
Future Pace:	Process of mentally practicing (rehearsing) an event before it happens. One of the key processes for ensuring the permanency of an outcome, a frequent and key ingredient in most NLP interventions.
Generalization:	Process by which one specific experience comes to represent a whole class of experiences, one of the three modeling processes in NLP.
Gestalt:	A collection of memories connected neurologically based on similar emotions.
Hard Wired:	Neurologically based factor, the neural connectors primarily formed during gestation, similar to the hard wiring of a computer.
Incongruence:	A state of being "at odds" with oneself, having "parts" in conflict with each other. Evidenced by having reservations, being not totally committed to an outcome, expressing incongruent messages where there is a lack of alignment or matching between verbal and non-verbal parts of the communication.
Installation:	Process for putting a new mental strategy (way of doing things) inside mind-body so it operates automatically,

	often achieved through anchoring, leverage, metaphors, parables, reframing, future pacing, etc.
Internal Representations:	Meaningful patterns of information we create and store in our minds, combinations of sights, sounds, sensations, smells and tastes.
Kinesthetic:	Sensations, feelings, tactile sensations on surface of skin, proprioceptive sensations inside the body, includes vestibular system or sense of balance.
Leading:	Changing your own behaviors after obtaining rapport so another follows. Being able to lead is a test for having good rapport.
Logical Level:	A higher level, a level *about* a lower level, a meta-level that informs and modulates the lower level.
Loops:	A circle, cycle, story, metaphor or representation that goes back to its own beginning, so that it loops back (feeds back) onto itself. An open loop: a story left unfinished. A closed loop: finishing a story. In strategies: loop refers to getting hung up in a set of procedures that have no way out, the strategy fails to exit.
Map of Reality:	Model of the world, a unique representation of the world built in each person's brain by abstracting from experiences, comprised of a neurological and a linguistic map, one's internal representations (IR). (see Model of the World)
Matching:	Adopting characteristics of another person's outputs (behavior, words, etc.) to enhance rapport.
Meta:	Above, beyond, about, at a higher level, a logical level higher.
Meta-levels:	Refer to those abstract levels of consciousness we experience internally.
Meta-Model:	A model with a number of linguistic distinctions that identifies language patterns that obscure meaning in a communication through distortion, deletion and generalization. It includes specific challenges or questions by which the "ill-formed" language is reconnected to sensory experience and the deep structure. These meta-model challenges bring a person out of trance. Developed in 1975 by Richard Bandler and John Grinder.
Meta-Programs:	The mental/perceptual programs for sorting and paying attention to stimuli, perceptual filters that govern attention, sometimes "neuro-sorts," or meta-processes.
Meta-States:	A state about a state, bringing a state of mind-body (fear, anger, joy, learning) to bear upon another state

	from a higher logical level, generates a gestalt state—a meta-state, developed by Michael Hall.
Mismatching:	Offering different patterns of behavior to another, breaking rapport for the purpose of redirecting, interrupting, or terminating a meeting or conversation.
Modal Operators:	Linguistic distinctions in the Meta-Model that indicate the "mode" by which a person "operates": the mode of necessity, possibility, desire, obligation, etc. The predicates (can, can't, possible, impossible, have to, must, etc) that we utilize for motivation.
Model:	A description of how something works, a generalized, deleted or distorted copy of the original; a paradigm.
Modeling:	The process of observing and replicating the successful actions and behaviors of others; the process of discerning the sequence of Internal Representations and behaviors that enable someone to accomplish a task.
Model of the World:	A map of reality, a unique representation of the world which we generalize for our experiences. The total of one person's operating principles.
Multiple Description:	The process of describing the same thing from different perceptual positions.
Neuro-Linguistic Programming [NLP]	The study of excellence. A model of how people structure their experience; the structures of subjective experience; how the person programs their thinking-emoting and behaving in their neurology, mediated by the language and coding they use to process, store and retrieve information.
Neuro-Semantics:	A model of meaning or evaluation utilizing the Meta-states model for articulating and working with higher levels of states and the Neuro-Linguistic Programming model for detailing human processing and experiencing, a model that presents a fuller and richer model offering a way of thinking about and working with the way our nervous system (neurology) and (linguistics) create meaning (semantics).
Nominalization:	A linguistic distinction in the Meta-Model, a process or verb turned into an (abstract) noun, a process frozen in time.
Outcome:	A specific, sensory-based desired result. A well-formed outcome that meets the well-formedness criteria.
Pacing:	Gaining and maintaining rapport with another by joining their model of the world by matching their language, beliefs, values, current experience, etc., crucial to rapport building.

Parts:	A metaphor for describing responsibility for our behavior to various aspects of our psyche. These may be seen as sub-personalities that have functions that take on a "life of their own"; when they have different intentions we may experience intra-personal conflict and a sense of incongruity.
Perceptual Filters:	Unique ideas, experiences, beliefs, values, meta-programs, decisions, memories and language that shape and influence our model of the world.
Perceptual Position:	Our point of view; one of three mental positions: first position-associated in self; second position-from another person's perspective; Third position-from a position outside the people involved.
Physiological:	The physical part of the person.
Predicates:	What we assert or predicate about a subject, sensory based words indicating a particular representational system (visual predicates, auditory, kinesthetic, unspecified).
Preferred System:	The representational system that an individual typically uses most in thinking and organizing experience.
Presuppositions:	Ideas or assumptions that we take for granted for a communication to make sense.
Primary levels:	Refer to our experience of the outside world primarily through our senses.
Primary states:	Describe those states of consciousness from our primary level experiences of the outside world.
Rapport:	A sense of connection with another, a feeling of mutuality, a sense of trust, created by pacing, mirroring and matching, a state of empathy or second position.
Reframing:	Changing the context or frame of reference of an experience so that it has a different meaning.
Representation:	An idea, thought, presentation of sensory-based or evaluative based information.
Representational System (RS):	How we mentally code information using the sensory systems: Visual, Auditory, Kinesthetic, Olfactory, and Gustatory.
Requisite Variety:	Flexibility in thinking, emoting, speaking, behaving; the person with the most flexibility of behavior controls the action; the Law of Requisite Variety.
Resources:	Any means we can bring to bear to achieve an outcome: physiology, states, thoughts, strategies, experiences, people, events or possessions.
Resourceful State:	The total neurological and physical experience when a person feels resourceful.

Satir Categories:	The five body postures and language styles indicating specific ways of communicating: leveler, blamer, placater, computer and distracter, described by Virginia Satir.
Second Position:	Point of view; having an awareness of the other person's sense of reality.
Sensory Acuity:	Awareness of the outside world, of the senses, making finer distinctions about the sensory information we get from the world.
Sensory-Based Description:	Information directly observable and verifiable by the senses, see-hear-feel language that we can test empirically, in contrast to evaluative descriptions.
State:	Holistic phenomenon of mind-body-emotions, mood, emotional condition; the sum total of all neurological and physical processes within an individual at any moment in time.
Strategy:	A sequencing of thinking-behaving to obtain an outcome or create an experience, the structure of subjectivity ordered in a linear model of the TOTE.
Submodality:	The distinctions we make within each rep system, the qualities of our internal representations.
Synesthesia:	A "feeling together" of sensory experience in two or more modalities, an automatic connection of one rep system with another. For example, a V-K synesthesia may involve perceiving words or sounds as colored.
Third Position:	Perceiving the world from viewpoint of an observer; you see both yourself and other people.
Time-line:	A metaphor for how we store our sights, sounds and sensations of memories and imagination; a way of coding and processing the construct "time."
Through Time:	Having a time line where both past, present and future are in front of you. For example, time is represented spatially as with a year planner.
Unconscious:	Everything that is not in conscious awareness in the present moment.
Universal Quantifiers:	A generalization from a sample to the whole population - "allness" (every, all, never, none, etc). A statement that allows for no exceptions.
Unspecified Nouns:	Nouns that do not specify to whom or to what they refer.
Unspecified Verbs:	Verbs that do not describe the specifics of the action—how they are being performed; the adverb has been deleted.

Uptime:	State where attention and senses directed outward to immediate environment, all sensory channels open and alert.
Value:	What is important to you in a particular context. Your values (criteria) are what motivate you in life. All motivation strategies have a kinesthetic component. This kinesthetic is an unconscious value
Visual:	Seeing, imagining, the rep system of sight.
Visualization:	The process of seeing images in your mind.
Well-Formedness Condition:	The criteria that enable us to specify an outcome in ways that make it achievable and verifiable. A well-formed outcome is a powerful tool for negotiating win/win solutions.

Endnotes

1   Luis Jorge Gonzalez, *Psychology of Personal Excellence,* Editorial Font, 1993[111]

2   Derek Copley, *Building with Bananas,* Paternoster Publishing[222]

3   Larry Crabb, *Effective Biblical Counselling,* Marshall Pickering, 1977[333]

4   quoted in *Churches with Roots,* Johan Lukasse, Monarch Publications, 1990[444]

5   John Seymour & Joseph O'Connor, *Introducing NLP (revised),* HarperCollins,1993[555]

6   Neil Anderson, *Rivers of Revival,* Regal Books, 1997[666]

7   Frank Farrelly & Jeff Brandsma, *Provocative Therapy,* Meta Publications, 1974[777]

8   Seymour, *op. cit.*[888]

9   Roger Ailes, *You are the message:* Dow Jones[999]

10 You can e-mail me for details on ifield4861@hotmail.com[101010]